★ **IF YOU SELL IMPURE FOOD**

★ **IF YOU MAKE UNSAFE AUTOMOBILES**

★ **IF YOU POLLUTE THE ENVIRONMENT**

★ **IF YOU EXPLOIT YOUR LABOR**

★ **IF YOU CHEAT YOUR CUSTOMERS**

Watch Out For Nader's Raiders!!!

The True Story Behind The Man Who
Created The Consumer Revolution

RALPH NADER:
A MAN AND A MOVEMENT

By Jay Acton and Alan LeMond

RALPH NADER:

A MAN AND A MOVEMENT

By Jay Acton and Alan LeMond

A NEW EARTH BOOK

PAPERBACK LIBRARY
NEW YORK

WARNER PAPERBACK LIBRARY EDITION
First Printing: December, 1972

Warner Paperback Library is a division of Warner Books, Inc., 315 Park Avenue South, New York, N.Y. 10010

To Jerry Gross and all other hard-working editors

Acknowledgments

The authors would like to thank their research assistant, Judith Ross, for her help. Also, those who helped prepare the manuscript: Mary Anne LeMond, Beverlee Galli, and Gail Acton. And last but not least all those who helped us by supplying information and by talking with us.

Contents

Ralph Nader:
A Man And A Movement

Introduction

1972. The lecture hall at Princeton filled early, but this night there was to be no lecture. It promised to be more like a revival meeting. Ralph Nader, consumer advocate and son of Princeton '55, had come to preach his gospel. It had been seventeen years since Nader left Princeton but there had been elements of Princeton that had never left him. His intense and disciplined work habits which he refined there, had helped spawn a half-dozen major pieces of legislation, not while he was on the floor of the House or Senate, but while he was in their galleries, an unequalled feat.

Thanks to Nader's persistence a major motor vehicle safety act, a wholesome meat act, a national gas pipeline safety act, a radiation control act, a wholesale poultry products act, a coal mine safety act, and an occupational health and safety act were enacted. The two regulatory agencies which most affect the consumer—the Federal Trade Commission and the Food and Drug Administration—both had high-level house-cleanings after investigations by Nader and his young associates.

Nearly an hour before Nader was to appear, every seat in the hall was taken. Many were Princeton students, some dressed in suits and ties, some informally—most notably one student in a hockey shirt and another in an expensive leather vest. The townspeople of Princeton had been invited to attend, and they did so in substantial numbers. There were families, high school students on a cheap date (no admission charge) and even a knot of teenyboppers in the balcony.

It would be the college students that Nader would be most interested in reaching this evening. If he could successfully motivate them and they in turn their younger brothers and sisters, consumerism would have made its way to all age groups. Nader sponsors a group of retired professionals (age fifty and over) in Washington, and his Nader's Raiders have ranged in age from seventeen to thirty-seven. Nader would also be especially interested in impressing these college students, for the Ivy League is where Nader has done most of his successful recruiting for his Raiders. To some this smacks of elitism, but a friend professes that the one thing that impresses Nader is "brainpower."

Thirty minutes before Nader's appearance and the audience is talking quietly. The first row of the hall has been reserved for those with tape recorders who don't want to miss a word of Nader's pronouncements, and for a few photographers who have put their equipment bags on the adjoining seat and are nervously fiddling with their cameras to make sure they won't miss the triumphant entrance.

Robert P. Walker, the head of American Program Bureau, Inc., Nader's lecture-booking agency, is the man who sees that Nader shows up at campuses like Princeton when he is supposed to. Nader has missed more than one speaking date because he missed a connecting flight or has been tied up with some pressing consumer matter.

It's Walker's job to soothe the ruffled feathers when this occurs and to get Nader his speaking dates in the first place. There is no end to the requests, but the time element is paramount. Walker refuses to say what Nader's top fee is, but he has been known to get $3,000 a lecture. Walker's organization gets about a third of Nader's take. Nader has spoken for nothing when he felt the cause was right, and if a law school can't afford his fee he will generally take a lower one. Two hundred lectures a year is not uncommon for Nader.

Of his esteemed client, Walker has said: "He's beautiful. He's honest. Uses every nickel he's got. Won't even buy a raincoat in the winter. Puts it into his investigations."

Finally, it is 8 p.m.; the appointed hour, and Nader, sans raincoat, is striding out onto the stage. Polite and sustained applause comes forth from the audience. Nader, shielding his eyes and smiling, takes a seat on the stage as the student who is going to introduce him goes to the podium.

Tonight there's a new twist. Nader will be debating Law Professor Henry Manne of the University of Rochester. The question before the house is: "Should the American Corporate System be Reconstructed?" Nader, of course, will handle the affirmative side of the question. He speaks first.

More sustained applause from the audience and this time a few whistles. After about a minute it subsides. Nader smiles briefly and then is off. His first few sentences are choppy. The material is familiar ground but tonight it seems to play tricks on him. He stops a couple of times and backtracks, rephrasing his words, as if to extract the proper essence. He has a sheaf of notes in front of him but he really doesn't need them, and he only looks at them as sort of a nervous gesture. He hunches over the podium, condensing his tall body as much as possible. His face is angular and his black bushy eyebrows are his most prominent characteristic. His dress is as bland as his speech style: grey suit, a blue shirt, an unfashionably-thin tie, and black shoes. He has a nineteen-cent Bic pen in the breast pocket of his suit jacket. His pants are cuffed and his shoes are plain.

No one is really listening to the words. They've heard the tune before and Nader makes no attempt to pep it up. The audience is mesmerized. They've come to see Ralph Nader perform and he's putting on a good show. He goes after business, he goes after the government, and he goes after citizens for not making the first two responsive to their needs. But easy does it on the citizens; after all, that's his constituency, and you don't bawl out your family in front of the enemy—Professor Manne.

Nader's humor tends to the ironic and is totally suffused with the fabric of his work. His best line, one that brings roars of laughter from the crowd and then applause, is when talking about the influence of DuPont of Delaware and the image of Delaware as a "corporate Reno": "GM would buy Delaware if DuPont would sell it to them."

Ten minutes into his presentation he is in high gear, marking his indignation with an outstanding number of facts, figures and illustrative examples. The juices are flowing now, Nader whistling his "s's" and rocking back and forth at the podium.

At the end of the twenty-minute opening statement he sits down to prolonged applause. Professor Manne has the unenviable task of defending the American corporate system. He carries it off with surprising good humor. But his assertions draw a series of animated boos from the pro-Nader audience. Nader and Manne exchange smiles. Manne is the fall guy in this routine and he knows it.

While Manne speaks Nader furrows his brows and rummages through one of those expanding file folders, extracting two or three pieces of paper. Close up one can see that even his sideburns are not modishly long. They are thin and cut off at mid-earlobe. His complexion seems sallow but the lighting is irregular and it's hard to tell. His hands are only average-sized but the fingers are extremely long and thin. On one wrist is a watch with a large dial and a wide leather band.

Professor Manne used his twenty minutes to go after Nader rather than to present his own side of the case. He parried a couple of times, seemingly striking paydirt on one occasion as he dug out some old Nader quotes from a 1962 magazine article, which on the surface does not seem to square with what Nader says now. Nader grinned, rotated his head once, licked his lips, as if to say, "Not bad, you've done your homework."

In his rebuttal Nader is much more animated. He waves his arms over his head, while making a series of intricate points. He exceeds the ten minutes allotted to him on this part of the program. The moderator slips him a note but he goes on like a car running red lights. Finally, he reaches a crescendo, and then withdraws, bowing his head. Nader knows how to milk an audience and this time he gets cheers, whistles and applause.

Professor Manne attacks but the battle is long over. He calls some of Nader's assumptions "naive," and says that Nader is only trying with his Raiders to impose a second layer of government. He criticizes Nader for not even having the foresight for hereditary disposition of the power he has appropriated for himself.

A brief question period follows after which Manne quips, "All my questions come from the left," meaning the left side of the hall. Nader hits back: "They're right." Applause and laughter and the evening.

On his way out Nader is buttonholed by a woman in her fifties. "I'm John's mother," she says. "Hey," says Nader, "we'll all have to get together. Drop me a line."

"But we're moving to Georgia," she says in desperation.

"Well," says Nader, "write me anyway."

"Where?" asks the woman. Nader gives her the address and she scribbles frantically.

Nader spends a few more minutes clarifying points of his talk but the people are more interested in just having a first-hand look than asking any substantial questions. Nader senses this and moves on. Outside, he gets into the back seat of an orange Maverick and to the dismay of the hangers-on is driven off.

What hath Ralph Nader wrought? Probably more than he ever dreamed of when he was growing up in sleepy Winsted, Connecticut, a small town about thirty miles northwest of Hartford. Since 1964, he has become the nation's favorite gadfly, leaping from imbroglio to imbroglio and spotlighting many of the country's most pressing problems. The name Nader has become a synonym for righteousness, selflessness and ascetism, as well as for getting action. As Butch Cassidy and the Sundance Kid would doubtlessly inquire: "Who *is* that man and what does he want?"

Nader was born the son of immigrant parents who built a successful restaurant-bakery business and who urged their children to be real citizens. Ralph and his brother once lobbied against parking meters being installed on Main Street in Winsted, and won. Their father, Nathra, a Lebanese immigrant, once told a reporter that his children had been brought up to "understand that working for justice in the country is a safeguard of our democracy."

Nader went to all the best schools, like Princeton, where he indulged a penchant for languages and majored in Oriental Studies. Besides English, Nader is conversant in Chinese, Spanish, Russian, Portuguese, and Arabic.

During the sleepy Eisenhower fifties, Nader attempted to enliven things. He tried to organize his fellow students to contest some of the more archaic rules which rotated classes through Princeton like clockwork. But in 1953, his classmates were busy planning corporate careers. Protests, sit-downs, sit-ins, and student participation were not to become part of campus vocabularies for another full decade. Nader protested against spraying the campus with DDT, which he claimed was destroying campus wildlife. For one of his courses he wrote a mini-critique of the Department of the Interior and the way it treated Indians. No one took Nader too seriously; after all there were plenty of fraternity pranks, goldfish-swallowing records and telephone booth stuffings to be done. Anyone who spent his time wondering about birds and Indians wasn't playing with a full deck.

Ralph Nader did not waste his time, however. He graduated magna cum laude, was admitted to Harvard Law School and proceeded to Cambridge to put himself through school. Nader drifted into the army after law school and finally set up a small private practice in

Hartford. It was during this time that his interest in auto safety crystalized. He began lecturing to small civic groups, all of whom responded warmly to his research, but they were unable to translate their verbal support into concrete action.

Frustrated, Nader left Hartford and moved to Washington, to see if by being closer to the action he couldn't effect some real change. MIT professor and former presidential-aide Daniel P. Moynihan, who had himself written on auto safety, got Nader a position in the labor department as a traffic safety consultant. Nader worked tirelessly, but all his words—written and spoken—went largely unheard until Senator Abraham Ribicoff of Connecticut, on the strength of Nader's work and a climbing highway death toll, decided to convene subcommittee hearings on auto safety. Nader left his labor post to work as an unpaid consultant to the subcommittee.

In 1965, a small New York publisher released a book called *Unsafe At Any Speed*, written by a relatively unknown lawyer named Ralph Nader. The rest, as they say, is history. The book sold a half-million copies in all editions and was translated into seven languages. Nader poured all his royalties, something over $50,000, back into his one-man crusade for auto safety, especially concerning himself with the Corvair.

Then he claimed that GM was spying on him, trying to get enough on him to blackmail him. GM blanched but later admitted this was true, and Nader received a public apology from GM chairman James Roche and $425,000 from GM in an out-of-court settlement, a kitty big enough to fund some of the consumer work he felt was most important.

Nader's continued nagging resulted in the passage and signing of the National Traffic Safety Act in 1966. Nader and his summer Raiders went after the Federal Trade Commission, the Food and Drug Administration, and the Interstate Commerce Commission, among others. The study group reports poured out. The summer Raiders were complemented by permanent staff members on such Nader-backed groups as the Center for the Study of

Responsive Law, the Public Interest Research Group, and the Center for Auto Safety, to name just three. About fifty full-time people work directly with Nader now; most are lawyers, and nearly all are professionals of one type or other.

But who is this man Nader? It would not be an exaggeration to say that the public and private Naders are intertwined. Nader works a twenty-hour day—reading reports, testifying before committees, speechmaking—and then repairing to his $80-a-month bedroom in a Washington, D.C. rooming house. His personal expenses are about $5,000 a year. Nader has no time for a private social life, because of his intense concern with creating a viable "social" life for the public. He is pressing for what he calls nothing less than a qualitative reform of the industrial revolution, a rather immodest goal for a man not normally given to excesses.

There are some, especially on the left, who claim that Nader is really just another reformer and nothing to get excited about. They argue he makes a virtue out of consumerism, just showing more people how to gorge themselves more effectively.

Nader *has* pressed for consumer reform—no question or argument there, but he's made everyone a bit more comfortable by doing so. He has forayed against those who are damaging our environment, appointing himself protector of the environment in which we live. In doing so, he has hit a more vital nerve; he has affected the quality of our lives in air and water pollution, for instance. He has fought corporate intransigence, Federal bureaucracy and Congressional indifference. Part of his weapon is his own inscrutable personal life—he is above suspicion. Part is his heavy reliance on the work ethic; part is the fact that he wins a lot, or at least appears to, and—make no mistake about it—winning is important to Americans.

To the young, he has become a symbol—something that middle Americans might want their sons to aspire to be. His admirers among the young, even those heavily into politics, are legion; and most of all, his Raiders, small though their numbers might be, offer a place for the most dedicated to work out their frustrations by putting their energies to constructive use.

Nader is not insensitive to the charge that he is a "meddling zealot." He once told a Congressional committee: "If I were trying to prevent cruelty to animals no one would question my motives, but because I happen to have a scale of priorities which lead me to engage in the prevention of cruelty to humans, my motivations are constantly inquired into."

Although Nader's conclusions have been attacked and assailed, his reports impugned and upbraided, he has never been sued for libel or slander.

How long will Nader keep it up? Certainly until that mythical day when he satisfies himself that all societal ills have been remedied, or more pragmatically, until his effect is muted. A 1971 Harris Poll had the populace for Nader by better than a 53–9 percent margin. (Thirty-eight percent were not familiar enough with him to comment.) By that margin, he's got to think he'll be around for a long time.

The question most asked about Nader's future concerns politics. Feminist Gloria Steinen and writer Gore Vidal both floated trial balloons about a "Nader for President" campaign. The response was encouraging. Would he accept a people's draft and take the plunge into the deep political waters? "No," said Nader, "politics is in such a low state of response it's necessary to go to the citizen to see if he'll wake up. Politics will improve when the citizen improves. Not only the average citizen, but the lawyer, doctor, teacher, engineer, the leaders as well as the followers."

The Young Mr. Nader

Nineteenth century Winsted, Connecticut, was a textile town. Some of the old mill buildings still stand on the town's main street but the textiles have long gone the way of the horse and buggy. Winsted is by most accounts a modest town. Its populace is about equally divided between blue and white collar workers. Its voting pattern is also pretty much split down the middle—half Republican and half Democratic, with a slight preference for the latter.

One of the highest hills in the town is the Nader homestead. It's a commodious ten-room white house complete with side porch and a backyard big enough to have a game of catch in. Located in an older part of town, one realtor estimated that the house—exclusive of the fact that Ralph Nader once lived there and his parents still do—would fetch $40,000–$50,000 in today's market. Behind the house, set even higher on the hill is a huge stone arch that says "Soldiers Memorial 1861–1865", commemorating those who died in the Civil War. The winding drive leading to the arch combines with its out-of-the-way character to make it a lover's lane.

Nathra Nader, the irascible eighty-year old patriarch of the Nader clan, emigrated from Arsoun, Lebanon in 1925, bringing with him his bride, Rose Bouziane. Nathra, a self-made man, had first come to the U.S. some six years before while still in his teens and worked at a succession of jobs on the East Coast. Having saved enough to support a wife, he married, and came back to the U.S., first settling in Danbury, Connecticut.

About two years later he moved to the country—Winsted—and opened a confectionary shop. One Winsted septuagenarian remembers the long-gone shop this way: "At first there was just a counter where they sold candy. Later I remember them adding a separate pastry part. Everything was always fresh and the Naders did a good business."

The sweet shop did well enough to allow the Naders to open a restaurant—The Highland Arms. The Arms was a Winsted fixture for some forty years, closing only in the late sixties when Nathra Nader decided to retire. Now a dry cleaning store and a clothing store occupy the space where the proud Arms once stood. A casual visitor walking along Winsted's Main Street would have no inkling, unless he knew better, that this had been where the Nader clan gathered.

The restaurant weathered several calamities. World War II forced hard times upon it, as did the destructive 1955 floods. Water reached the five-foot level in the main dining room. The Mad River toppled most of the buildings on the other side of the street. Today, Winsted remains a town with only one side of its main street. John Slocum, associate publisher of the *Winsted Evening Citizen* says that he seems to recall a fire in the restaurant which forced still another remodeling. He's not precisely sure of the date but thinks it might have happened in the late thirties or early forties. For one of the restaurant's renovations the Naders engaged an Oriental-American architect whose decorating ideas were not congruent with Mr. Nader's. The loud and long "discussions" that ensued amused the more conservative New Englanders passing by. It was completed, of course, and business resumed as usual.

One did not go to the Highland Arms for peace of mind or, according to several of the town's citizens who are unwilling to be named, for haute cuisine. Nathra Nader was and is a man of strong opinions. His views on what he considered to be the pressing issues of the day were prix fixe—part of the meal, and no extra charge was made for them. Unfortunately, there was more than one soul who gave up going to the restaurant, not because they couldn't stomach the food but because they didn't like to be berated each time they sat down to a repast. To Nathra Nader, democracy was to be practiced and espoused at one's place of business as well as at home. The restaurant was one forum for public events; the dinner table at Hillside Avenue was another. If the Naders lost a customer now and then because of their outspokenness, they certainly didn't let it affect them at home. All four of the Nader children: Claire, five years Ralph's senior; Laura, two years younger than Claire; and Shaffik, four years older than Ralph, participated. Dinnertime in the Nader household was a kind of "My Weekly Reader" pageant brought to life. There was no formal agenda but all the children were expected to contribute their opinions—and back them.

Two virtues were sacred in the Nathra Nader scheme of things: hard work and love. It was more important for one to expend all energies in the things he believed to be right than to not care at all. It was important, even though disagreeing with people on principles and ideas, to still treat them as human beings—with care and compassion.

Ralph's older brother Shaffik had a grating personality which ran very much against the Yankee temperament. In conversation at the restaurant and at the Winsted Town Meetings, Shaffik was often quite vehement in defending his position. He was physically different from his father and his brother—squat and heavy-set, with a brooding disposition and a fixing stare. "With all due respect," said a Winsted Town Meeting regular, "it was

Shaffik's manner that put people off. He was quite an intense man and people often mistook that intensity for arrogance."

John Slocum adds: "I must confess that at first I was not very convinced when Shaffik brought up the idea of a community college in the town. We're a Yankee community and we tend to take our time to assess things. Shaffik saw that the time had come for a community college. It was a bitter battle and Shaffik finally had his way. It was a good thing; I'm grateful for his persistence. My son went there." The whole Nader clan was big on education. Claire went to Smith, and received a PhD in sociology from Columbia. Laura Nader attended Wells College and Harvard Graduate School. She teaches anthropology at Berkeley now. Ralph went to Princeton, then on to Harvard Law School.

Shaffik's community college was housed in the old Gilbert School, from which all four Naders had graduated. Today, Northwestern Community College has added a pair of modular wings to the main structure and some 1,200 students attend the accredited two-year school. Inside the small school there is a peculiar air of lassitude which somehow does not do justice to the Nader energy which spawned it. The bulletin board in the basement has no notice of consumer or environmental causes save one plea from a Nader group in Hartford—an event which took place months ago. No one bothered to remove the sign. Otherwise, the board has the usual notes: an alto sax for sale, a ride to Boston needed, a room in an apartment up for grabs.

Nader is remembered as a quiet youth by those who taught him in grammar school and high school. After school one was more likely to find him reading a stack of old *Congressional Records* than playing basketball on a street corner. One classmate was journalist David Halberstam, who was later to win a Pulitzer Prize for his reporting from Viet Nam. Halberstam had nailed down his award before the public had even heard of Ralph Nader. There are two main recollections of Ralph in Winsted. Those who knew him and the family and who often frequented the Highland Arms remember him as friendly and easy-going, a contrast to the querulous Nathra and his older son. Those who weren't that well-acquainted with the family (they would probably be in the minority since even today the population is only 11,000) recall him as simply quiet and colorless. A good kid, maybe a whit too serious, but certainly a boy who was not going to get in trouble.

The Gilbert School is Winsted's public secondary school. It is named after an old Yankee watchmaker, William Gilbert, whose company supplied many a job in town until the early sixties, when it ceased operations. Gilbert's bequest paid for the high school education of each child in town until the late forties. The new Gilbert School is merely a short walk from the Nader house. Today all but two of the school's students are from Winsted, for the school is no longer in a position to accept out-of-towners as they once were.

The 1951 *Miracle,* the school's yearbook and so named because of the frenetic and disorganized activity which produced its first volume, shows Ralph in a conservative suit with hair just slightly shorter than it is today. His mien is serious, but his eyes let on that he is slightly bored by the proceedings. His face is fixed with a hint of impatience, almost as if he were urging the photographer to hurry up and get the whole thing over with. Under his picture is the notation: "Anything for peace." Nader was further defined by his classmates as "quiet and smart." He could be found "at home or in the restaurant." His only extracurricular activity was the dramatic club in which he participated all four years, although none of his roles are listed.

"Spud" Fecto, assistant headmaster of the Gilbert School, remembers him as "a good solid student, but not a premier one." This is borne out by the *Miracle* which records honors for three of his four years. He participated in no sports. "Even though he was tall, he was gangly and had no coordination. I also don't think he was particularly interested; that probably had a great deal to do with it," said Fecto. He further observed that Ralph really had no social problems. He was simply not an extrovert. "He was just a pretty quiet kid who used to carry a briefcase around." Fecto was not the only one who noticed his omnipresent briefcase. Nader's classmates impishly had him leave it in the class will to—of all things—a girl. They rated his character as "egotistical," his pastime as "studying," his dislike as "women." These characteristics may or may not be applicable, but they certainly made a mistake when they predicted his future as the corporate executive: "the man with the briefcase."

It would be wrong to say that the town is taken with the idea of Ralph Nader as Public Hero Number One. Says John Slocum: "If they were to announce that Ralph Nader was coming in on the bus tonight, I'd be surprised if anyone but his parents met him. Now Steve Blass, who lives in a nearby town and pitched for the Pittsburgh Pirates in the World Series, came here and was mobbed. I guess it all depends on what a town considers its heroes to be. Ralph is respected here but Steve Blass is a hero."

In two Main Street shops which carry paperbacks, neither *Unsafe At Any Speed,* Nader's masterwork damning the Corvair car to obscurity, or any of Nader's spinoff study group reports were to be found. In the town's small library where Nader did a good deal of his reading and studying, *Unsafe* is not even listed in the meager catalogue, though it does list a 1969 book by Laura Nader from the University of California Press called *Talea and Juquila.* Two early Nader Raiders' reports are listed. A close look at the shelves will, however, uncover two copies of *Unsafe,* one a gift copy from an unknown donor. The library has no collection of Nader memorabilia on display. In fact, there is nothing in the entire town that casual visitors would chance upon indicating that Ralph Nader had lived his first seventeen years here.

Nader came back to give the commencement address at the Gilbert School in 1970. The auditorium was packed, but many in the audience felt what Nader had to say, outside of describing his own experience growing up in Winsted and attending the school, went over most of the students' heads.

Ralph Nader could relocate himself permanently back to Winsted and he would be left to his own devices. To the man with a passion for personal privacy, this would be ideal.

Ralph Nader narrowed down his choice of colleges to a handful of Ivy League schools. Two reasons probably prompted him to opt for Princeton over one of the others. First, he could feel comfortable in its small-town suburban atmosphere. Princeton could be likened to an upper-class Winsted. Secondly, it had the things he wanted to study: Far Eastern languages and Foreign Relations.

The Princeton of the early Eisenhower years was a sleepy place compared to the turmoil on college campuses of the late sixties. Conformity was the order of the day. Beer bashes and good times were hailed. The ideal was to become the corporate executive—"The Organization Man"—and lead the country club life. Ralph Nader, Spartan, could not have chosen a less likely place to study. Even now in the seventies a kind of placid air surrounds Princeton. It is a self-contained world and it took Nader a few false starts before he finally found his own footing there.

It is often mentioned that H. H. Wilson, a professor of political science at Princeton, has been one of the biggest influences on Nader and his work. He remembers the young Nader as an excellent student in the courses he took. Perhaps even more significantly, he recalls Nader as a man "intellectually excited" by his studies, something even rarer for these times than for college students today. Nader seemed impressed by classroom lectures during the time he studied under Wilson, who describes one class session as follows: he went to a local drugstore and bought a can of hairspray which had supposedly been banned the year before, and a cigarette lighter. In class he then dramatically demonstrated why the hair spray was banned: when he lit the lighter near the spray, flames shot up. This product, despite its ban, remained on the market. The issue of the uninformed and unprotected consumer was brought to light.

Another professor, Steve Slaby, points to Scott McVay, now an assistant to the Dean at Princeton, as a close friend and perhaps another influence on Nader. McVay is singularly uncommunicative about what role he might have played in Nader's development. He will only refer all questioners "to the man's [Nader's] work."

Wilson feels that Nader's incentive and strength of character is almost totally due to his family background. "The story of how his father made the restaurant successful, and how the kids were taught to revere the American way of life, has been related to me. They were raised to serve the country in an honest way."

Both Slaby and Wilson wonder about the net effect of Nader's work. They feel, and many critics will agree, that by working within the system Nader is not necessarily going to succeed at changing it as much as he would like to. Secondly, that this working within the system helps to support it rather than truly alter it. And finally, that the system and the men in it are corrupt and sooner or later will get him. If and when Nader has true power, it will only take one small misuse of it to put him in even more disfavor with the powers that be. That's when the government/corporations groups will go after him in earnest.

Despite the radical attitudes of these men, they admire him very much. However, not all the people at Princeton do. Some feel he is bucking the system and don't like that idea. Others feel he is simply going around from project to project yelling "fire" and not putting any of them out. A number of professors have wondered why, with a six-figure income, Nader lives the way he does. It's because the style of life and the things that are associated with money of that sort just do not interest him, but it is hard for some of the Princetonians to understand that.

In February of 1972 the 16th annual Woodrow Wilson

Award was conferred on Nader. It is given to the alumnus "best typifying the motto 'Princeton in the Nation's Service.'" At thirty-eight, Nader is the youngest Princetonian ever to receive it. The Award, presented before 1,600 persons at the alumni luncheon, carried with it a stipend of $1,500, roughly half of Nader's usual speaking fee. Said Princeton President Robert Goheen, "He has rocked boats and displeased many, but because of his determined and persistent efforts, we may look forward to more safety on our highways and in our mines and in our factories." In his acceptance speech, Nader noted, "When I was a freshman, student dissent consisted of refusal to wear white buck shoes and a freshman beanie." On a more serious note, he said the existence of corporate malfeasance "generates a much higher moral imperative to act when the resources and knowledge are present."

The reception accorded Nader was polite but not overwhelming. The *Daily Princetonian* made mention of the fact that several people left when the award was presented to Nader. All claimed their departure was unrelated to Nader's acceptance of the award.

H. H. Wilson sees Nader on the average of once or twice a year. He doesn't feel that Nader has undergone any personality changes since his days at Princeton—he still very much goes his own way. Wilson doesn't pretend to know what Nader's social life was like at school but seems to agree with the general impression that Nader was a loner, partially because he was more interested in his studies. Another professor who also taught Nader, Professor Melvin M. Tumin of the Department of Sociology, concurs with Wilson and the general concensus. "He didn't go out. He never went to parties or the movies." Nader himself has refuted the antisocial picture of himself at Princeton. "Students were very anti-intellectual in those days. You'd be studying in Firestone Library and people would come in from Prospect Street and yell 'dirty grind.'"

Nader took six courses a semester instead of the usual five and discovered that the only way to finish all the work was to stay awake half the night studying. Another anecdote of Wilson's is about a mysterious light burning late at night in the library which turned out to be Nader studying—he had snuck in through the windows. Such student conscientiousness was rewarded with a key to the library doors. He must not have begrudged the extra work, however, for he has been known to say that on the whole "Princeton was really pretty good to me." Besides the open and available stacks of the library, the accessibility of his teachers and the prevailing academic philosophy helped to enhance his stay.

Many courses were taken on audit. "I wasn't always interested in my regular courses," he admitted. A classmate, Benjamin "Red" Zelenko, says that Nader's late hours occasionally put him in the academic doghouse. "He slept through classes in the morning," said Zelenko. "Once he got a note from his Chinese professor saying 'Nader-san, the midterm exam is next week and you better show up for it.' " Nader remembers sleeping through his first class—Classics—and looking at the sundial next to the building thinking "What a way to start Princeton." And in fact that class was one of three courses that Nader received a below-average mark in.

While still at the University Nader studied quite a bit of Arabic language and history. His senior thesis was a 208-page report entitled "Lebanese Agriculture", which advocated increased help from the government for the people. Nader studied Oriental languages intensively but his application to take a special three-year program in that specialty was refused because of "inadequate grades." While in the Woodrow Wilson School of Princeton, he attended several conferences, including one on Puerto Rico taught by Melvin Tumin. Nader loved the course fieldwork in Puerto Rico and has since become a great advocate of fieldwork courses in general. Tumin thinks that Nader got more in two weeks in that country than most people would have in a lifetime of traveling. It was most helpful that Nader was fluent in Spanish, one of the five languages he speaks.

Many students attend Princeton on scholarships, even those whose parents were a good deal better off than the Naders. Nader didn't. But then Nathra Nader wanted it that way, feeling it was almost un-American to have someone else pay the freight. Nader was fond of hitchhiking to and from school, boasting that he had never once paid for a ride home during his stay at Princeton. He did make use of a fellowship received for studying conditions in Arizona, New Mexico and California, part of a program on agricultural problems in Europe.

Nader made two outward stabs at dissent. One was a protest to the school newspaper about the free use of DDT on campus. He finally confronted the editors after his letters were consistently not being printed. Didn't they know what it was doing to the birds, didn't they know what it was doing to themselves? But cries went unheeded. His other gesture was to join the Prospect Cooperative Club, the only one of Princeton's eating clubs that did not have servants.

Graduating in the top ten percent of his class in 1955, Ralph was accepted into Harvard Law School for the fall semester, and he decided to head out west for the summer, working as a cashier in Yosemite National Park. Sometime in August the Highland Arms was wrecked by the 1955 floods. Nader saw a newspaper picture of the ravaged restaurant and, unsuccessful in attempts to reach his family, made his way home immediately. They were all right, but the restaurant needed to be entirely rebuilt.

In September, Nader headed north to Cambridge, Massachusetts and Harvard. If Princeton had stirred him to greater academic heights, Harvard had just the opposite effect. He has often referred to it as a high-priced tool factory. Harvard University and Cambridge itself are pressure places. Closer to the realities of urban living, one either sinks or swims. Nader and his habits fell outside the normal run. One could still be an individual at Harvard, but it was with the risk of alienating others. In sum, Nader was a law student who chose to get mediocre grades. Irrelevant classes were skipped in order to attend those of interest, regardless of requirements. The traditional goal of finishing high in the class and landing a Wall Street job did not interest him at all. His journalistic talents were put to use, however, in writing two well-remembered articles for the school's newspaper. *The Record.* One was on the status of Puerto Rico as a commonwealth, the other on the treatment of the American Indian. By his senior year Nader had become the editor-in-chief, but left in a dispute over the type of paper it was to be printed on. Probably the most salient tidbit to be culled from the rather dreary Harvard Law School curriculum was a paper Nader wrote called "Auto Negligence Design and the Law." This paper was to serve as a springboard for his best-selling book *Unsafe At Any Speed.*

In June 1958, Ralph Nader graduated from Harvard Law School. Neither a corporate job nor a clerkship with a federal judge lay ahead.

Armed with a baccalaureate degree from Princeton and a law sheepskin from Harvard, Ralph Nader did the unusual once more. He joined the Army. During six months active duty at Fort Dix in southern New Jersey, his new occupation was cook. Despite its requirement that he rise each morning before dawn to prepare grub for thousands of his fellow soldiers, Nader is said to have enjoyed his brief army stint. After this period he was placed in the inactive reserve for five years.

The years 1958–1963 are almost lost years in Nader's life. He had reached out in many different directions but the net effect of his projects was negligible. No one had heard of him. No one really cared, with the exception of his family, about what he was doing.

Nader's first article on auto safety in a major national magazine appeared in *The Nation* in April of 1959. Called "The Safe Car You Can't Buy," it incorporated the best thinking on auto safety available. Other articles on this topic appeared in 1963 and 1965 in this magazine.

Nader toured several Scandinavian countries during the summer of 1961. Impressed by the use of ombudsmen to resolve disputes between the government and individuals, he tried without success to get an ombudsman bill through the Connecticut state legislature. At least two states today do have some form of ombudsmen as Nader envisioned them, even though the concept as a whole never caught on. This had been his main focus when more material on the auto safety crisis came to the fore.

The spring of 1963 found Nader touring South America with a friend. By sending back dispatches for the *Christian Science Monitor* and *The Atlantic,* he received enough money to finance his trip. Next Nader did some general legal business, handling cases involving personal injuries, divorces, wills, contracts and the like, but it was not very satisfying work. Nor was his part-time job teaching history and government at the University of Hartford from 1961 to 1963. By testifying before the Connecticut and Massachusetts legislatures later in 1963, he tried to arouse some interest in getting seat belts put into automobiles, but by and large he spoke to empty houses. Polite silence greeted his entreaties to business and service organizations.

John Slocum, the associate publisher of the *Winsted Evening Citizen,* was at that time working for the *Hartford Times.* He recalls several visits from Nader during those years. "He'd be quite friendly and tell me what he was doing. He was pleasant enough to be with. But I guess none of us could ever have thought what the upshot of all this activity was going to be."

Red Tape & "Unsafe At Any Speed"

Imagine Ralph Nader, dark, disheveled, very intense, showing up at various government offices, the unsettling fire of pure conviction burning in his dark eyes, spouting fact after fact to a compromising Congressman or Senator. Speaking of corporate tyranny (from which the Congressman's campaign coffers were filled) and speaking of the criminal neglect of safety engineers and corporation presidents. Talking about the people's rights and the consumer's need to know, the necessity of government protection for the consumer and—horror of horrors—demanding that the government regulate the automobile industry.

Imagine him showing up at Bobby Kennedy's Justice Department determinedly searching for evidence that the auto industry might be guilty of anti-trust violations. The same auto industry that had generally supported John F. Kennedy for President.

"Five or six years ago, when I went to Washington," said Ralph Nader to Sam Blum in a 1971 *Redbook* interview, "the quickest way to get a politician out the door was to talk about consumer protection. It was taboo. Now politicians are beginning to run campaigns on consumer and environmental issues."

And some—Nader could have pointed out—have built their national reputations on just such issues. Witness the case of Senator Edmund Muskie, with whom Nader was one day to have a difference of opinion concerning pollution control. But that was much later, and in early 1964, Nader would have given a great deal to have Muskie, or any other Senator, give his opinions the serious consideration they deserved.

Nader might have been using a figure of speech when he said "the quickest way to get a politician out the door was to talk about consumer protection," but it is also highly likely that it actually happened.

For Ralph Nader was making waves. And there's nothing worse to any politician than a stormy sea, because the politician, like a captain, once launched on a cause (as Nader so zealously preaches that all politicians should be) would often go down with his ship. Especially if that ship were engaged in battle against the corporate giants of America. One has to look at realities. One has to compromise. What could one congressman do? What could one man do?

Nader, of course, was soon to answer those questions.

At the age of thirty, Ralph Nader went to Washington, a carpetbagger from Connecticut, and his carpetbag was filled to overflowing with information, conviction, and a driving need to do something about what's wrong with this country. His first aim was auto safety.

Nader didn't just wander into Washington with no place to go, he was invited to come by Daniel P. Moynihan, a close confidant of the Kennedys and also the Assistant Secretary of Labor for policy planning. Moynihan had joined the Labor Department staff because he felt that here was an opportunity to bring to government attention the fact that vehicle design does play an important role in the nation's highway slaughter. As part of that attempt, he asked Ralph Nader to serve as a consultant on highway safety. Nader was to be paid $50 a day, and his main assignment was to prepare a report on the "Context, Condition, and Recommended Direction of Federal Activity in Highway Safety."

The report would end up to be a veritable tome, a 234-page, double-spaced, detailed study with ninety-nine pages of notes. It was laboriously researched, minutely documented, and tremendously damning to the Detroit auto makers.

The need for such a study had been building for a long time. The ever-rising death tolls—in spite of many publicly and privately supported driver education campaigns—were seizing many Americans with a deep sense of guilt and frustration. In fact, almost every American could name a friend or a member of their own family who had been involved in a serious auto accident.

There were already in existence some traffic safety departments and organizations such as The National Safety Council, The American Automobile Association, and The President's Committee for Traffic Safety. But these were ineffective at best, Nader pointed out, and at worst were actually representing the manufacturer rather than the public.

The President's Committee for Traffic Safety, Nader said, was composed of thirty-seven people, mostly representing automotive, insurance, transportation, and "professional" safety associations, and that most of the money to run the bureaus was contributed by outside "interest" groups such as The Automotive Safety Foundation and The Insurance Institute For Highway Safety. (And besides that, they were illegally using the Presidential Seal on some of their correspondence, Nader reported to Moynihan, who was delighted at the news. It was not a major point about highway safety, but one that might cause the executive branch's interest in PCTS to increase, Moynihan thought.)

Nader also emphasized that all the energy and direction in highway safety had gone into blaming the driver for accidents, and, in effect, trying to create a safer driver rather than a safer car. The "Let's Make A Safer Driver" campaign was the industry's chief cry and self-indulgent promotion program in 1964, and it is still heard today.

In the February, 1972, issue of *Road and Track,* engineering editor Ron Wakefield wrote a special article on automotive safety. In the article, "Automotive Safety: where we're going and some of the problems we face," he began with a question which could have come directly from the automobile company's promotion mill:

"What would you, *R & T* reader, sporting-car enthusiast, practitioner of skillful and fast driving, do when you needed a new car in 1980, if the only new cars available were huge, super-heavy and super-expensive sedans designed specifically to crash into a solid barrier at fifty mph without killing you? Would you happily give up your old sports or GT, light and maneuverable, economical of fuel, conservative of space and natural resources, entertaining to drive and esthetically satisfying, for the new machine whose greatest attraction is that it can save you from the worst crash you can imagine having? Would you be willing, in short, to give up all your automotive pleasure for utter risklessness?"

This has long been the industry's cry, but Nader says that a safe car does not have to be a tank, does not have to be esthetically unpleasing, or super-expensive, that Detroit has the skill and means of designing a light, maneuverable and—because of mass production—economical "safe car." "Make money and the public be damned," Nader has indicated is the auto industry's attitude.

In the *Road & Track* article, Wakefield went on to say that the main thrust of safety legislative programs "has always been, and continues to be, the automobile itself. Not the driver, who is acknowledged to be the real culprit."

In answer to that article, W. R. Kittle, Chrysler Corporation Director of Vehicle Safety and Advance Control, wrote a congratulatory letter which was printed in the April 1972 issue. "I strongly support your contention that 'driver skill development is a worthwhile, necessary goal.' . . . Keep up the good work; we will do our best at this end. I would like to see your article get wider circulation. Is this possible?" (The ABC audited circulation figure for *Road And Track* was 307,873 at the time the article was printed.)

Nader was fighting this same attitude back in the early sixties. He contended that the idea of trying to create a safe driver rather than a safer car was not a realistic one. As Nader ponited out, "Safety measures that do not require people's voluntary and repeated cooperation are more effective than those that do . . . Furthermore, our society knows a great deal more about building safer machines than it does about getting people to drive safely."

It had all been said before by scientists and safety research teams, but little had been done about it. In the early fifties, some university-supported studies had proven the effectiveness of seat belts. But it was not until Representative Kenneth Roberts began a 1956 House investigation into the matter that Detroit began to offer seat belts as options.

Perhaps that gave Nader a stronger incentive to complete his highway safety report for Moynihan, in hopes that it would be used as a basis for an even more comprehensive Congressional investigation into the auto industry and highway safety. In any event, he felt that his report would be helpful toward that end. But Nader was wrong.

The report was effectively shelved, and the reason why it was has to do with the way things work in the nation's capitol.

When Nader came to Washington, he was not naive, by any means, but he was idealistic. He believed that Congress could be effective, that Congressmen and women were responsive and responsible representatives of the people, that Congress was capable of leading the nation rather than dragging their collective heels, or at best walking several steps behind. And because Nader didn't know he couldn't get things done, he got things done. Maybe not exactly as he wanted them done—with not as much teeth in the laws as he thought necessary—but still he achieved more than anyone had previously thought possible. His report might have been shelved in the Labor Department, but that certainly didn't stop him. He went on from there, and he has been pushing and pulling and needling the government to action ever since.

Moynihan probably didn't realize what he was starting when he asked this virtually unknown highway safety expert to become his background consultant. He didn't realize he was helping to create a modern Robin Hood, a champion of the people.

Moynihan and Nader had been aware of each other since 1959, when their two articles on highway safety had appeared in the same month in two different magazines. Nader's article, "The Safe Car You Can't Buy," appeared in *The Nation* on April 11, 1959; Moynihan's "Epidemic On The Highways" in *The Reporter,* April 30, 1959. Nader read Moynihan's article while he was serving his six months active duty as an army cook at Fort Dix, New Jersey. The two began a correspondence and it was soon evident that they shared a strong conviction, namely that something must be done about the senseless slaughter on the highways.

As Nader pointed out in *Consumer Reports* in January, 1966, more than 49,000 Americans were killed on the nation's highways in 1965; 1,800,000 were injured but not disabled. As both Moynihan and Nader were acutely aware—and more people should have been—this was an unforgivable waste of lives, time and money.

Moynihan's approach to the solution of this problem, as evidenced by his writings and his actions, was more in line with established views than was Nader's. Moynihan's approach was lighter, professorial in tone, somewhat wittily academic, while Nader's attitude and actions were blam! hard-hitting, emotional and obviously, convincingly determined. Moynihan was concerned—and very commendably so—but Nader . . .

Nader was an auto-safety freak.

The fifty dollars a day which Nader received for his work as consultant was thoroughly earned—every penny of it. He was a tireless worker, even though he didn't keep regular hours, and sometimes didn't show up at his office for days. He preferred working alone at night, when the building was deserted. His desk was piled high with paperwork—notes, scraps, and books. He was given a great deal of latitude in his work; so much in fact, that Moynihan and others in his office have said that often no one was quite sure just what Nader was doing.

But one thing everyone in contact with Nader knew, and that was Nader was thoroughly concerned with highway safety. He spent hours searching through government records, talking with government employees and generally familiarizing himself with all aspects of highway safety.

In *Citizen Nader,* author Charles McCarry related that Moynihan's wife, "who was Nader's hostess at a number of dinner parties, eventually stopped inviting girls to keep him company. Nader ignored them and talked of nothing but cars. He thought the nation should be in a rage because the automobile had killed almost three times as many Americans as all the wars in U.S. history."

Auto safety dominated his every action.

When his report was finished in the spring of 1965 (which he had to research twice, since the first time he lost his notes in a Washington taxi), the point he was to make was that since all aviation, marine, and rail vehicles and equipment must adhere to public safety standards, why should the automobile industry—alone—have such unparalleled independence? And his recommendation was to "request legislation to establish a Federal Highway Transportation Agency as a separate administrative body directly responsible to the President."

Since the report was not meant to be read, actually, it never was. It was meant to be a background document for Moynihan's reports and proposals to the various departments and executive branches. If Moynihan needed proof or backing up—he had the report.

However, Moynihan's way was not Nader's way; and the Moynihan who at one time had said, "One out of every three cars manufactured in Detroit ended up with blood on it," was to prove less effective than the dynamic young consumer advocate who said, "When and if the automobile is designed to free millions of human beings from unnecessary mutilation, these men, like their counterparts in universities and government who knew of the suppression of safer automobile development yet remained silent year after year, will look back with shame on the time when common candor was considered courage." (From *Unsafe At Any Speed)*

Nader did call Moynihan "the first political scientist to devote attention to auto safety," but Nader was the first to become a political force, and to transform criticism into action. And Nader's first appearance as a political force came about because of the Ribicoff Subcommittee.

In December, 1964, Senator Abraham Ribicoff read an article which referred to a book called *Accident Research: Methods & Approaches.* The article and the book made Ribicoff realize for the first time that the car itself was a factor in vehicle accidents. It was enough to compel Ribicoff, who was a chairman of the Senate Subcommittee on Executive Reorganization, to prepare the background material for a Senate hearing on the issue of auto safety. It was this famous hearing that brought the name Ralph Nader into the awareness of the American consumer.

When Nader became aware of the existence of the Subcommittee work, he dropped in on Jerome Sonosky, staff director and general counsel of the Subcommittee. Nader and Sonosky hit it off at once, and after a long conversation, Sonosky realized what a tremendous boost Nader would be for the preparation of the background material. Not only was he knowledgeable, and willing to work hard, but he was willing to work for nothing and, more importantly, he was willing to let the Senators take credit for what he did.

"That's not modesty, just tactics," Nader was to say later in a 1968 *Playboy* interview. "If I can get three Senators to say something, it's better than for me to say it." It certainly was true, in early 1965, that if a Senator made as grave a charge as wanton neglect against the auto industry, it would be much more effective than if Ralph Nader made it. Who was Ralph Nader, anyway?

After it was all over, it became very apparent that Ralph Nader was the one man who made it all possible. He delivered his reports to the Subcommittee containing hard facts, logical recommendations, righteous outrage.

He also testified very persuasively at the actual hearings. But it was his escapade with General Motors that topped it all—that provided the necessary catalyst. For the idea of a private citizen being hounded by one of the largest corporations in the world, of having the gall to pry into someone's private life just because he dared to criticize the corporation was enough to arouse even the most jaded of Senators to action.

But, previous to this, the groundwork Nader had laid made it possible for him to take every advantage of the situation provided by the GM gaffe.

Among the little-known facts Nader turned up in the course of his research was that since 1965 the Detroit automakers had been recalling cars because of safety defects. The recalls were managed as quietly as possible, with little or no publicity. It was difficult for members of the Subcommittee to believe this, but when they did look into the matter, they found that since 1960, almost eight million cars had been the subject of one of 426 recalls, most of which had been in areas of great safety hazards, such as brakes, steering and suspension systems.

Nader, in his testimony and his writings at the time, was to make such hard-hitting statements as:

"While [the auto industry] properly states that safety features have to be proven before adoption, it exempts such features as sharp fins, glare-ridden chrome, hardtops, wraparound windshields, undersized tires, smaller brake drums, and front placement of fuel tanks in rear-engined cars."

And, "a newly designed rear end on a car costs its maker at least twenty-five million dollars, more than the total auto industry expenditure on collision research in fifteen years."

He also pointed out that while existing public agencies had supported some research that was university-based, "with few exceptions (the seat belt being one), these studies never yielded any policy recommendations affecting the vehicle."

Nader, of course, was not the only one who, during the hearings, made pointed and emotionally packed statements. John T. Connor, then Secretary of Commerce, said in November of 1965 that "death on the highway does not come at the end of a meaningful life. It can come at any moment . . . Between the ages of five or thirty years, motor vehicle accidents are the leading cause of death. More than one-third of all highway victims are in this age group."

All of these statements—Nader's, Connor's and others—were leading toward what Nader considered the most important point of all: The auto industry could not and should not be allowed to police itself, for no matter how much lip service was paid to the problem of improved safety in vehicle design, all that had been accomplished was a relating of what could not be done, and no suggestions were offered as to what could be done.

The government had tried a minor type of auto-industry regulation in 1964, when the General Service Administration (GSA) was created by Congress with the authority to set safety standards for government purchased vehicles. It was hoped that this would force the industry to adopt these standards for all the cars produced, but according to Nader, the standards finally published by GSA were abysmally inadequate. In a February, 1966, issue of *Consumer Reports*, Nader wrote: "Of sixteen automobile makes built between 1953 and 1959 that were tested by John Swearington of the Federal Aviation Agency, nine would have met or exceeded the present GSA requirement without padding. Swearington considers all sixteen excessively dangerous."

In defense of GSA, however, Nader said that Congress was much to blame. They had created the agency without sufficient funding. "No special appropriations were made available to facilitate the hiring of expert consultants by GSA."

The hearings were in progress when Nader surprised both Moynihan's office and the Subcommittee staff with the publication of his book *Unsafe At Any Speed.* Few were that impressed, however, as other people had written books, including some of the staff, and it certainly wasn't surprising to them that Ralph Nader had authored a a book whose subject was auto safety. Nader told the Ribicoff committee that he had been thinking about such a book since 1960, but the way in which he actually got the assignment was almost an accidental one.

It has been said that Nader's idea for *Unsafe At Any Speed* was turned down by several publishing houses before it was finally accepted. But that is not exactly true, according to Richard Grossman of Grossman Publishers in New York, who did publish Nader's book.

"There was no book," Grossman says. "Ralph planned to write a book. And it is true—which has been quoted in one of the books about him by Buckhorn—that he wrote a letter to Random House, to which they replied that they couldn't see how a book like that could be successful unless one of the insurance companies got behind it.

"Another house sent him a letter saying that they were just not interested. That's all that was proposed to other publishers.

"The fact is that I read an article by James Ridgeway called 'The Corvair Tragedy' in the *New Republic,* which so incensed me and outraged me that I went after Ridgeway to write the book. He said he wouldn't, because he didn't feel qualified, but that a man named Ralph Nader was, so I went after Nader."

When Ralph Nader first came to talk to Grossman about *Unsafe At Any Speed,* in September, 1964, the publishing house was located in a basement brownstone office in lower Manhattan. Nader's advance against royalties was only $2,000, not a lot, but Grossman was a new and struggling company.

During the writing of the book, Nader and Grossman worked together very closely. There were times when the editor (Grossman edited it himself) and the writer would hole up in a hotel working furiously on the book. "It wasn't just a weekend, it was many, many nights and days. It's not uncommon for editors to work closely with authors, especially with authors who have masses of material and need a sounding board. An example is when you have a great number of cases and want to demonstrate one particular point. The other person has to help winnow out material to see which fits.

"Also, we shared a belief that the book was going to

be an important one. [For that reason I worked on it more closely than any other book.] It had to be right—there couldn't be any mistakes, no typographical errors, no misquotes. And that takes a lot of doing. It had to say what Ralph Nader wanted it to say and the way he wanted to say it. If my opinions as an editor didn't jibe with his opinions, we talked it out for a long time."

Certainly much of Nader's research for the Labor Department's 200-plus-page report helped him when it came to writing the book, but the book was written in a different style than the report; Nader was aiming at two entirely different audiences. The report had been written for experts, but the book was for the consumers. Nader wanted the American public to realize what was being done to them and he wanted them to become angry enough to do something about it. *Unsafe At Any Speed* was the first major book in the field of auto safety to bring to the attention of the American people how they were being taken. Published almost simultaneously with Nader's book, however, was another published by Random House called *Safety Last*. "It was by Jeffrey O'Connell," Grossman says. "The co-author's name was Arthur Mayer. It didn't get much attention because Ralph's book was by far the deeper, more detailed, and more profound book, but essentially its theme was the same.

"Certainly in the field of auto safety, Nader's book was the thing that unplugged the mass of dissident energy that consumers had about the quality of products that they are paying money for. It launched Naderism. It spawned the National Highway Safety Act of 1966 as well as a proliferation of consciousness about the fact that the second collision of a car was the fault of the car. . . . The real thesis of the book is that it is about engineering and design, not about people. It isn't interested in what causes accidents; it's interested in making crash-worthy vehicles. That is an industrial concern as vehicles are manufactured by industries for consumers."

Unsafe At Any Speed was anything but subtle. It was hard-hitting, emotional, and an unprecedented blast at the Detroit complex of automakers. General Motors was especially hard hit. In the first chapter of the book, Nader all but sealed the little Corvair's doom.

An adaptation of that first chapter, which was printed prior to publication in *The Nation* (November 1, 1965), said in no uncertain terms that there was something very wrong in the way the little car handled. He opened with an example of what had happened to one victim. "In August of 1961, Mrs. Rose Pierini lost her left arm when the 1961 Chevrolet Corvair she was driving turned turtle just beyond the San Marcos overpass on Hollister Street in Santa Barbara, California. Exactly thirty-four months later, in the same city, General Motors decided to pay Mrs. Pierini $70,000 rather than continue a trial which for three days had threatened to expose on the public record certain driving characteristics of their brand-new automobile."

The adaption was not in the least unfaithful to the book. The same Panzer-tank prose boomed out. In his preface, Nader used words such as *death, injury, inestimable sorrow, deprivation, mass trauma, new and unexpected ravages by the motor vehicle.* All emotion-packed and lethal. But the book was packed with much more emotion (although McCarry said the book was read more for tone than for text); it was filled with fact after frightening fact.

The title of Chapter One was "The Sporty Corvair: The one-car accident." Nader simply demolished the car, which had been so warmly received by most of the American automobile writers. He detailed with startling precision what he called the "tragedy of the Corvair—the strong oversteering tendency of the design. And he emphatically believed that GM had been guilty of neglect in producing and selling to the public an automobile that was especially vulnerable to "one-car accidents." Or, as Nader put it, "one of the greatest acts of industrial irresponsibility in the present century." He stated that since October, 1965, more than one hundred suits alleging instability in the Corvair had been filed around the country.

While he did detail the case of Mrs. Pierini, who won her case when GM settled, he did not detail at least one of the cases GM did win. So it was no wonder that *Life* magazine reported in a 1966 issue that Detroit felt the book to be inflammatory and one-sided, "like a prosecuting attorney's summation to the jury."

The point was, of course, that Nader was not trying to be "fair," he was trying to save lives, and his "summation to the jury" was as pointed and as heated as it would have been had he been arguing to save an innocent man from death row in an actual court case.

The Corvair was not the only object of Nader's attack. He exposed the whole attitude of the automobile industry—what he called a "We *feel,* therefore we do not research" attitude. This basic operating procedure, Nader said, applied not only to safety research and standards, but to pollution control as well. A good example of this attitude was regarding the efforts to curb the emissions of oxides of nitrogen. "This ingredient, which is as dangerous to the public as carbon monoxide or any of the other hydrocarbon series, has been largely ignored, and the industry has refused to offer any cooperation with people interested in the problem." He ripped into the engineers, the stylists, the traffic safety establishment, and—to a lesser extent—Congressional attention to vehicle safety.

Unsafe At Any Speed was by no means all criticism. He also listed proposals as to what could be done to further the reality of a safe car. Among these proposals was the idea of a passive restraint for the automobile passengers. He suggested that "a kind of inflatable air bag restraint" might work better than seat belts because such a system does not depend on the active participation of the people in the car. With seat belts, the driver and passengers have to put them on. If this is not done, of course, the belts are ineffective. With air bags, the protection is automatic. A sensing device at the moment before impact would cause a large airbag to inflate and cushion the passengers against the crash, and especially the "second collision," which is where the head strikes the dashboard, the steering wheel, or the windshield. The controversy over use of air bags continues even now.

But Nader was then and continues to be an avid supporter of the system.

But the proposals, as good as they were, did not hurt nearly as much—or catch the public's attention as much—as did the sweeping attacks. But in spite of Nader's attacks, the quiet from Detroit was deafening.

"The book got a lot of attention for us," Grossman says. "We're a very small house. But it got a lot of attention from us as well. I went around the country talking to newspaper editors because I anticipated that the editors might be approached by the newspaper advertising departments and be asked not to review the book. The advertising departments would be doing this on the grounds that they get an awful lot of advertising from the automobile industry and the subjects of this book put them in an unfavorable light, which might offend them.

"So I decided to take a trip and went to Washington, Richmond, New Orleans, Dallas, Houston, Denver, San Francisco, Santa Barbara, L.A., and Chicago. And I said, 'Look, I don't care if you blast the book. I'm not trying to lean on you to give it good reviews. But do not, by any means, knuckle under to pressure not to acknowledge it. Pay attention to it. It's important.'

"They did pay attention, by and large. One editor, now retired, blatantly told me outright: 'I wouldn't touch that book at all. Do you think I want the newspaper publisher coming at me?'

"*Life* magazine said they wouldn't touch it with a ten-foot pole. And they didn't.

"The book didn't sell like crazy, but it sold well enough, got serious reviews, and was paid attention to."

The book wasn't widely reviewed, at first; but where it was, it was generally well-received. *The Wall Street Journal* said the book was "powerful and persuasive," *Road Test* magazine called it "required reading," and in Detroit, "practically every auto executive has a copy of Nader's book on his desk and when they discuss it they can rarely avoid raising their voices," *Life* reported in an article on auto safety in 1966.

Meanwhile, during these early on-sale months of

Nader's only self-authored book, the Ribicoff hearing continued. And the industry continued to parrot the same familiar phrases they had always used. Industry spokesman, Karl Richards, who was a veteran representative of the Automobile Manufacturers Association, said it this way: "Driver improvement offers the greatest hope for traffic safety."

And Nader fought back. In doing so, he voiced one of his earlier indications of a coming disillusionment with Congress when he said, "There is considerable danger of Congress enacting the 'no-law' law for automobile safety." The "no-law" law, he explained, is ambiguous and/or makes no mention of enforcement . . . "Provides no standards for balanced representation on advisory committees . . . does not consider the issue of indiscriminate adoption of private safety standards, requires no periodic progress report to Congress on administration and enforcement, does not stipulate that prescribed standards must be technically justified in writing that is publically available, restricts authorizations for funds to a nominal or zero level, and is peppered with the word 'discretionary' as to the promulgation and issuance date of standards."

Nader had good reason to worry. Take the case of a previous hearing held by the Federal Trade Commission in January, 1965, on the safety of the automobile tire, and continued by the Senate Commerce Committee the following May.

"One tire manufacturer stated that 'over the years, vehicle manufacturers, in an attempt to cut costs, have cut down the amount of tire they are designing into their vehicles, and that some vehicles are overloaded when they are empty," FTC Chairman Paul Rand Dixon told the Senate Committee. The actual culprits, according to the hearings, were the vehicle manufacturers, but they chose not to come to the hearings to testify. Why not? Why not, indeed. Any administration knows the power of the auto industry, and its great influence on this country's economy. Not only in the hiring of thousands of workers in the factories and offices, and in the selling of autos, but in the fact that they purchase vast amounts of steel, lead, rubber, zinc, aluminum, and upholstery leather.

It's nice to be so important. It's safe and secure. And if you happen to be General Motors with fifty percent of the market, it's even nicer.

"What's good for this country is good for General Motors, and vice-versa," said Charles E. Wilson on January 23, 1953. His statement summed up the "big corporation vs. the people" attitude nicely. Wilson was chairman of GM at the time and had been nominated by Eisenhower to be Secretary of Defense. Wilson was asked if he, as Defense Secretary, would be willing to make a decision against GM: Therefore, his answer. It seemed to tell a lot about the men who worked for GM, not only then but later, in 1966, when the idea of industry responsibility for auto safety reached a climax.

Ralph Nader was becoming a nuisance to the giant corporation, for "big businessmen . . . like to present themselves as public-spirited citizens; it is therefore at least embarrassing and often costly to have Nader come along and prove that behind some of the handsome institutional advertising there may be dangerous products, a depleted environment, and shoddy ethics. Quite naturally, some big businessmen think of Nader as a dangerous radical," Sam Blum wrote in *Redbook.*

And if GM thought of Nader as a dangerous radical, then wasn't it only right to bring that fact to light and blunt Nader's criticism that GM was symbolic of much that is wrong with American society?

Some men at GM thought so, and "Affair GM" began.

Affair GM

It is a favorite game of Nader-watchers, especially with those who are not completely enamored of him or his methods, to suggest reasons why Nader has remained in the public eye as long as he has—he was created by the press," some suggest; and others claim that Naderism is simply a fad. These people then go on to predict his future demise. Like any phenomenon in any field—from rock music to politics, the Beatles to Edward Kennedy—Nader's fame has suggested his downfall. The Beatles broke up with a touch of bitterness, and almost everyone knows the tragedy of Edward Kennedy. There must be a Chappaquiddik in Nader's life, mustn't there? Every hero has feet of clay, an Achille's heel.

Then what is Nader's weakness? The people who are looking for that fatal flaw are growing in number every day that he continues to defy their laws of nature.

An editorial in the *New York Times,* March 30, 1972, which was an adaptation of an article from the Harvard Law Record by Bob Hernandez titled "The Lurking Danger of Naderism," proposed that Naderism "stifles creativity and self-assertion by providing easy compromises between desire for power or financial security on on hand and conscience on the other, *ultimately ignoring that only selflessness and pure dedication to people can bring change.*" (Italics added.) Surely, of all the criticisms of Nader and Naderism, that is the most incredible. If Nader is not selfless and dedicated then there is no way to describe him.

And back in 1966, General Motors found that out—much to their dismay.

"I read *Unsafe At Any Speed* when it first came out. Like most Americans, I first became aware of him as a symbol of the consumer movement when he got involved in that controversy with General Motors . . . I knew he was an author and critic of the automotive industry but not much more than that until the GM controversy," said Robert Pitofsky, Director of the Federal Trade Commission's Consumer Protection Division, in March, 1972.

Maybe if it hadn't been for the GM affair, Ralph Nader might have had a harder time becoming the prominent consumer crusader that he is, but that is purely hypothetical. The fact is that the GM affair did happen, and because of it Nader received a lot of sympathy and a great deal of attention. Sometimes it seems nothing is real to the visually-oriented American public unless it is on our movie or television screens. And what GM did for Ralph Nader was to cause a close-up of the Nader profile to appear on our image screens and make him real for us.

The GM affair went something like this:

On January 10, 1966, not quite two months after his book appeared on the stands, Ralph Nader felt that someone was watching him. He was in Des Moines, Iowa, at the time, having gone there to testify as a traffic safety expert at the Iowa Attorney General's request. There was nothing concrete that Nader could put his finger on, but there was this man at the Hotel Kirkwood, where Nader was staying, that he remembers seeing two or three times. The presence of the man bothered Nader. He felt uneasy, but he shrugged it off.

Then, a month later, on February 10, Nader was scheduled to appear before the Ribicoff subcommittee to testify, again on behalf of auto safety. A few days before this appearance, Nader began to receive strange calls late at night from voices identifying themselves as being with Pan American or Railway Express. They were just nuisance calls, until late one night he received one call where a hostile voice said: "Why don't you go back to Connecticut, Bubby-boy!" Nader, naturally, was concerned.

The Friday after he testified before the subcommittee, Nader was scheduled for a television interview in the Senate Office Building. Two men, apparently following him, lost him at the elevator, and looking confused, caught the attention of the guard. What were they doing in the Senate Office Building? They were following Mr. Nader, they told the guard. The guard advised them to leave, and later the incident was reported to Nader.

Now, of course, Nader had no doubt—if indeed he ever had—that someone for some reason had caused him to be placed under surveillance. The natural finger of suspicion would point at the auto industry, since Nader's book was now causing some stir, and he was testifying at various auto safety hearings. Besides that, several of his articles criticizing the auto industry had appeared in various national publications.

Before the Senate Office Building incident, Nader had told some of his friends about his feelings of being followed, and of the phone calls. And probably, like most of us would, his friends found Nader's story hard to believe. A crank caller, maybe? A little paranoia, maybe? That doesn't happen in America. Nader was working too hard. Anyway, until the incident, Nader had little to offer as proof. Now he knew.

Meanwhile, the actual investigation into Nader's private life was going full blast. Nader's landlady was contacted and asked about her roomer's credit standing; Nader's stockbroker, also. Harold Berman, a professor at Harvard Law School for whom Nader had once worked as a research assistant, was contacted. Thomas Lambert, Jr., editor-in-chief of the American Trial Lawyers Association, for whom Nader had written some articles, was asked questions about Nader.

There were several other incidents as well. Nader was followed from Philadelphia to Washington. A reviewer who had written a laudatory review of *Unsafe At Any Speed* was asked about Nader. The lawyer to whom Nader dedicated his book was approached and asked questions.

In all, something like sixty of Nader's friends and relatives were interviewed, always under the pretext of a pre-employment investigation for a very good position as a researcher and writer for an unnamed party. The inquiries were about his sex life, his social life, his financial status, his political beliefs, his racial prejudices . . . Was Nader an alcoholic? A drug addict? What did he do in his free time? Where did he get his money? Did he like girls? Was he an anti-Semite?

This last question was based on the flimsy excuse that he was of Lebanese extraction. And the questions about his sex life were based on the fact that he was over thirty and not married. (Well, also because of the fact that his high school yearbook had said, in typical high school fashion, that Nader was a woman hater.)

Legitimate reasons for legitimate questions? Maybe, if you believe that using detectives for surveillance to find out about someone's private life is okay. And if you believe that a giant corporation like GM has the right to try and find "something" to pin on their most vocal critic to discredit him.

There were also two other incidents that occurred during this period when Nader was under surveillance, which were never sufficiently explained away. One occurred on February 20, on a Sunday evening in a drugstore near Nader's Washington rooming house. A very attractive brunette approached him, asked him if he would care to join her and some friends at a private discussion of "foreign affairs." Nader declined the invitation, saying that he was from out of town, and the girl left.

Then a few days later on the 23rd of February, a stunning young blonde approached Nader in a Safeway Supermarket also near his home. Would Nader be so kind as to help the lady move a heavy object into her apartment? No, Nader was late for an appointment. And without asking anyone else in the market—although there were several others there—the girl left.

Were these girls sex lures, trying to trap Nader into a compromising position? Nader thinks so. GM and the detectives involved deny it. It is interesting to speculate, though, that someone might have thought that since the brunette didn't work, maybe Nader preferred blondes.

In any event, Nader had enough to give the story to a fellow writer, James Ridgeway (the man who had first been offered the auto safety book by Grossman), and Ridgeway broke the story in the *New Republic*. His article, which appeared in the March 12, 1966 issue, was titled "The Dick," and pointed a questioning finger at the auto industry.

The story was also broken a few days before *The Nation* came out in an issue of the *Washington Post* by reporter Bryce Nelson. Nelson, who resembles Nader somewhat, claimed that the detectives had also followed him one day by mistake. This was strongly denied by the head of the investigating agency, but considering the fact that the whole investigation had a Keystone Kops flavor, it made the "wrong man" incident palatable to most other people involved.

The story was picked up by the other papers and word of the investigation had now reached General Motors. President James Roche, on the spot because of the wide publicity, began to cause the wheels to turn inside the corporate structure. He must deny the accusation before GM's public image was tarnished. Ford and Chrysler had already issued statements denying that they were involved. He asked that a statement to the press be issued denying any involvement between GM and the Nader investigation.

But Roche had a surprise coming. "In the process of ordering a formal statement denying our involvement, I discovered to my dismay that we were indeed involved," he was to state later at the hearing. So the wheels had to turn a different way. Now a statement would be issued which would admit the GM involvement, but also detailing the "legitimate reasons" for that involvement.

Late at night on March 9, 1966, General Motors issued this formal statement to the press:

"General Motors said today that following the publication of Mr. Ralph Nader's criticisms of the Corvair, in writings and public appearances in support of his book *Unsafe At Any Speed,* the office of its general counsel initiated a routine investigation through a reputable law firm to determine whether Ralph Nader was acting on behalf of litigants or their attorneys in Corvair design cases pending against General Motors. The investigation was prompted by Mr. Nader's extreme criticism of the Corvair in his writings, press conferences, TV, and other public appearances. Mr. Nader's statements coincided with similar publicity by some attorneys handling such litigation.

"It is a well-known and accepted practice in the legal profession to investigate claims and persons making claims in the product liability field, such as in the pending Corvair design cases.

"The investigation was limited only to Mr. Nader's qualifications, background, expertise, and association with such attorneys. It did not include any of the alleged harassment or intimidation recently reported in the press. If Mr. Nader has been subjected to any of the incidents and harassment mentioned by him in the newspaper stories, such incidents were in no way associated with General Motors' legitimate investigation of his interest in pending litigation.

"At General Motors' invitation, Mr. Nader spent a day at the GM Technical Center, Warren, Michigan, early in January, visiting with General Motors' executives and engineers. He was shown a number of engineering and research testing and development programs in the field of automotive safety. A number of the accusations in his book were discussed at length, and a presentation was made of the evidence used in the successful defense of the only two Corvair lawsuits tried.

"Mr. Nader expressed appreciation for the courtesy in providing him with detailed information, but he nevertheless continued the same line of attack on the design of the Corvair in a number of subsequent press conferences, TV, and other appearances. This behavior lends support to General Motors' belief that there is a connection between Mr. Nader and plaintiffs' counsel in pending Corvair design litigation."

(As to the timing of the GM statement, which was issued very late at night—a trick sometimes used when one does not wish a rebuttal to appear in the same edition of a newspaper—Robert Kennedy said that it reminded him of President Kennedy's remark about dealing with the politically sensitive disclosure of his choice for Attorney General: "I'll open the door at 2 a.m.," said the President, "and say, 'It's my brother.' ".)

The next day after GM's statement, Senator Abraham Ribicoff tore off a telegram to Roche. "Am announcing on Senate floor today that Subcommittee on Executive Reorganization will hold hearings March 22 on Nader-GM matter. Respectfully invite your attendance as a witness."

Ribicoff was angered by the fact that the investigation appeared to be aimed at harassing a subcommittee witness; he was to remind General Motors that there is a federal statute which allows a five-year prison term and $5,000 fine for anyone who attempts to intimidate a Congressional witness.

The stage was now set for the public reprimanding of GM. Not that GM had done anything that different from other "routine" investigations by governments and corporations. But GM had been caught.

"It is beneficial to explore the workings of such a routine investigation and its framework of operation," said Ralph Nader at the hearing. "People all over should know that things like this go on so that they can, quite apart from laws, apply the customary social sanctions in a community which can operate to discourage or stifle such probings. But unless some definitions and sharpened values appear soon in our nation to limit such inquisitorial excesses, the employment of this essentially arbitrary power will continue its undermining of individual expression."

The hearing was held in the mammoth Caucus Room of the Senate Office Building. The principals—Roche and his attorney Theodore Sorenson, Senators Ribicoff and Kennedy (all except for Nader, who was late) were silhouetted against the white marble walls. The Caucus Room was jammed with reporters, cameramen, and private citizens. It was as if that Washington circus of the fifties—the McCarthy hearings—had come back to town.

Exactly at ten, the time set for the hearings to begin, Ribicoff rose and faced the assembled multitude:

"I have called this special meeting today to look into the circumstances surrounding what appeared to be an attempt by General Motors Corporation to discredit Mr. Ralph Nader, a recent witness before the subcommittee. This large company, whose principal executive officers appeared before this same subcommittee last July, has admitted responsibility for undertaking a determined and exhaustive investigation of a private citizen who has criticized the auto industry verbally and in print.

"There is no law which bars a corporation from hiring detectives to investigate a private citizen, however distasteful the idea may seem to some of us. There is a law, however, which makes it a crime to harass or intimidate a witness before a congressional committee. One of our purposes here today is to inquire into the purposes and effects of the action initiated by General Motors."

Nader still hadn't shown up. He was, in fact, standing on a street near his boarding house, trying futilely to hail a cab. Probably at that moment Nader wished he owned a car.

Meanwhile, back at the hearings, Ribicoff had called a recess, in hopes that Nader would show up. He wanted Nader to be the first witness. But by 10:15, when the star witness had not appeared, Ribicoff called James Roche to the stand.

Roche came prepared to apologize. "I deplore the kind of harassment to which Mr. Nader has apparently been subjected. I am just as shocked and outraged . . . as the members of this subcommittee. I am not here to excuse, condone or justify in any way our investigating

Mr. Nader. To the extent that General Motors bears responsibility, I want to apologize here and now."

Roche went on to admit that it was an understatement to say that he wished he had known about it earlier, and he intended to make certain that he was informed "of similar problems of this magnitude in the future . . . such errors will not happen again. It . . . has not been and will not be our policy . . . to undertake the surveillance or broad background investigation of those persons who write or speak critically of our corporation and our products."

However, Roche denied that GM had any intention of intimidating Nader, or hindering his testimony before the subcommittee. And the girls Nader claimed were used as sex lures were not a part of the investigation. Neither were the late night phone calls. In the end, he apparently convinced the committee that he was upset about the whole affair.

Roche's apology and humble manner before the subcommittee was not shared completely by Aloysius F. Power, general counsel for General Motors, who had ordered the investigation in the first place. Power denied that the investigation was harassment of Nader, but eventually conceded that he was "not proud" of his part in the sordid affair.

"The decision that an investigation of Mr. Ralph Nader should be undertaken was made by me in the discharge of my responsibilities as the general counsel of General Motors," said Mr. Power at the hearings.

He said that at the time the investigation was instigated, there were 106 lawsuits against GM totaling approximately forty million dollars in damage claims. "Were the Nader articles and his forthcoming book part of an organized nationwide publicity campaign to pre-try the Corvair cases by television, newspaper, and magazine, and to precondition prospective jurors in the cases still to be tried throughout the United States?"

Power, conceiving the idea that Nader was connected with the damage suits, started a preliminary investigation about the time Nader's book was published in November, 1965. This investigation failed to turn up any usable information other than the fact that Nader had once lived in Connecticut and now probably was living in Washington. Wanting more information on Nader than this, Power had a member of his staff, Eileen Murphy, contact Richard Danner, a Washington lawyer and former member of the FBI, asking Danner to get in touch with a good detective agency for a more intensive probe.

Danner testified before the committee that Eileen Murphy had furnished him with all the information she had concerning Nader, including a copy of an investigative report "covering some activities in Connecticut and some background data that she apparently compiled from press, magazines, and other publications. She also related to me other facts and matters for investigation. Miss Murphy stated that it was strongly believed by her and the legal department of GM that Mr. Nader was in some manner connected with or working for the plaintiff's attorneys in the Corvair negligence suits against General Motors, but that no compelling proof of this had been adduced as yet."

If indeed this were the real reason for the GM investigation, Nader had countered this problem earlier in the year. While at General Motors in February, Nader had assured GM that he had no connection with the Corvair cases. And in the February 10, 1966 issue of the *New Republic* he was quoted as saying: "There is absolutely nothing wrong with representing clients in cases against Corvair. But I am not representing any clients in Corvair cases and never have done so."

Danner contacted Vincent Gillen, also a former FBI agent, who runs an investigative agency in New York. Gillen, taking the job, in turn subcontracted two other detective agencies in Washington and Boston to handle some of the field work. The investigation began in January.

Gillen sent his agents a straight-forward memo: "The above-mentioned (Ralph Nader) is a free-lance writer and attorney. Recently he published a book, *Unsafe At Any Speed,* highly critical of the automotive industry's interest in safcty. Since then our client's client has made some cursory inquiries into Nader to ascertain his expertise, his interests, his background, etc. They have found out relatively little about him . . . . Our job is to check his life and current activities, to determine 'what makes him tick,' such as his real interest in safety, his supporters, if any, his politics, his marital status, his friends, his women, boys, etc., drinking, dope, jobs—in fact, all facets of his life."

Gillen claims that he tape-recorded the entire conversation with Danner, and in that conversation Danner asked him to find out: "What are his motives? Is he really interested in safety? Who are his backers, his supporters? How does he support himself? Who is paying him, if anyone, for this stuff?" Danner also revealed the name of the client, General Motors, to Gillen and said, "If we handle this right, both of us will get a lot of business from them."

As the investigation proceeded, Gillen filed his reports on an almost weekly basis beginning on February 7, 1966, to Danner, who in turn sent them, unedited, to Eileen Murphy at GM.

These reports eventually turned over to the subcommittee contained about ninety-six pages, mostly containing aspects of Nader's private life and little if anything about his connection with the pending Corvair litigation.

When Gillen took the stand at the hearings, he defended his position and the investigation. Many of the personal questions concerning his sex life and his racial prejudice were in his words "in fairness to Ralph."

"What the hell's this 'fairness to Ralph'?" Senator Kennedy asked sharply. "You have to keep running around the country proving he's not anti-Semitic or queer? Ralph's doing all right."

Ralph certainly was doing all right. Not only had the incident outraged the Senators because here was a great corporation out to clobber a guy because he wrote critically about them, but Nader's private life proved to be spotless.

"You and your family can be proud," Ribicoff told Nader. "They put you through the mill and didn't find a damn thing against you."

It must be the vulture instinct in Americans to want to tear apart that which is alive and vital; to watch and wait for that fatal mistake and then close in for the kill. "If I am so imperfect," they seem to be saying, "then you are, also. Tell me what makes you imperfect. Greed for money? What *are* you getting out of your crusade on my behalf?" Maybe that's why scandal sheets do so well, and gossip columns and movie magazines. (Does Ralph Nader really meet that well-known Hollywood starlet secretly and double-date with Henry Kissinger?)

In a *Science* magazine article, April 1, 1966, Nader said of General Motors executives: They "continue to be blinded by their own corporate mirror image that it is the buck that moves the man. They simply cannot understand that the prevention of cruelty to humans can be sufficient motivation for one endeavoring to obtain the manufacture of safer automobiles."

Yes, it probably was hard for GM executives to understand that, as difficult as it is for most of us to understand that. For to many people it is incomprehensible that anyone would choose to live as Nader does; as almost an ascetic, a monk. He seems to show no especial interest in food, beautiful women, or other sensual pleasures. Everybody has such interests at some time or another. We all know that. Can Nader's only vice be that he has a sweet tooth, especially for cookies?

Robert Fellmeth, a friend of Nader's and a co-worker, now heading the investigation of Congress, says that yes, Nader's image as an ascetic is a true one. The reason GM didn't find anything which could be used against him derogatorially was because there was nothing to find.

"Okay, I'm different than he is," Fellmeth says. "I love sex, I love good food. I love to drink . . . sensual things. I believe in leading a balanced life. But I believe while working with Nader at least eighty percent of my life is directed toward that work. I work fifteen to twenty hours a day. This has been going on for three years now and as long as I'm working with him I'll feel that way. But when it's done, I'll return to a balanced life."

Nader isn't like that, Fellmeth continues, and "the reason is . . . well, take an athlete in training; he spends an enormous amount of time practicing and if he loves it, even more. And Ralph is like that, loving and involved in something that most people do not find an interest in . . . research, reading, academic things. He finds those things interesting. Fascinating!

"That's the way he was brought up. There's no compulsion driving him to save the public or anything. He just loves doing that kind of work. A true intellectual, he loves learning."

And then a pause. A bit of Fellmeth philosophy: "You know . . . sex is an acquired thing. If once I got past adolescence and had not done much sexually, I would probably not be very interested in it. And if I were very much interested in something else, I would probably not think of it very often—not knowing what I was missing type of thing."

Then back to concrete examples of Naderisms: "For instance," Fellmeth continues, "if I say I'd sure like to go down and lie on the beach for a while, he'll say, "Well, there's the sun. It's the same sun. Instead of taking two days going down to the beach, why don't you take two hours and lie on a bench right here? There's the sun. There's no difference.' And he's right. The difference is psychological. And he doesn't have that same psychological thing; that escape kind of thing. He doesn't have to escape because he's right where he wants to be. He has an advantage also in that he does a variety of things in his work—giving speeches, reading, talking with people, writing, being involved with legislation . . . a mixture of things, whereas most people are doing just one thing and get tired of it sometimes. I think more and more Americans are going to turn to this way of life, seeing a model that's attractive . . ."

Maybe so. It would be nice if more people enjoyed their work, but still, to live like Nader, that's hard. He can't be for real. There must be something Fellmeth doesn't know about him.

But that's today, after Nader has achieved fame. Back in 1966 no one was thinking that way. Except for someone caught in the corporate structure of that giant, GM. And because someone at GM thought that way, the thought and the subsequent action became a landmark in the lives of both Ralph Nader and the American consumer. And probably, also, in the life of General Motors as well.

The Special Subcommittee hearing which was over in that one day raised some very bothersome questions, among which was: what right had General Motors or any other big corporation to pry into a private citizen's private life? And did they indeed have that right?

Ribicoff had pointed out that there was no law against this. The only legal basis for the hearing to determine the extent of the probing into Nader's private life was that there was a Federal law against intimidation of a government witness. Senator Kennedy at the hearings said:

"I think you [General Motors] were justified, if you felt for the protection of your company, your stockholders, and the good name of the automobile, the Corvair, and felt justice on your side, to conduct an investigation of the kind to determine whether Mr. Nader was in fact in the employment of some of these litigants and that there was an effort, a conscientious, organized effort, to try some of these cases in the newspaper rather than to try them in the courts, and from what I have learned, there has been some of that effort in the Midwest and some on the West Coast rather than just doing it through the courts.

"There have been a good deal of public statements in connection with this matter. So I understand your concern. I can understand the fact that you would feel an investigation to determine about Mr. Nader's connection and association with these individuals, particularly if he was going to be an expert witness, was completely justified. That part of it I don't find any fault with."

What Kennedy did question was "whether that investigation went on to the area of harassment, intimidation, and possibly blackmail. There are some of the questions that were raised by the investigators. I think this is a matter that is of concern to us and to the general public."

There was no evidence proven at the hearings that GM had indeed intended to blackmail Nader, or that they hoped overtly to intimidate him. But how many men, with lesser dedication than Ralph Nader and a less-spotless private life, would continue to pursue a campaign against GM and the rest of the auto industry? It is not hard to answer this question.

And besides that, the fact of the investigation itself, which GM had publicly announced with the formal press statement before the hearings, was a slur by intimidation. "Had it not been for the hearings," the Senators pointed out, "the record would not have been set straight."

But the record was set straight and Nader was exonerated.

Among some of the lighter aspects of spying which came out of the hearing was the fact that the investigators had not even found out whether or not Nader had a driver's license. Nader helped Gillen's investigation out immediately afterward by showing him his Connecticut license.

At the end of the hearing Ribicoff ended with a somber note. "There is too much snooping going on in this country. People don't seem to believe that others have a right to privacy."

Nader's encounter with GM had a positive effect, however. For much credit must be given to Nader, if only because he caused some Senators to feel that if a large corporation could be so insensitive to individual rights, then "to hell with them!" The resultant passage of the Traffic Safety Act required the establishment of Federal Safety standards for all vehicles sold after January 31, 1968.

It was a definite victory for Nader; the previous bill—which before the Nader-GM hearing seemed set to pass Congress—had a leisurely timetable, which could cause, as Ribicoff pointed out, "fifty million new cars [to] roll of the assembly lines free of any safety regulations."

Nader, of course, agreed with Ribicoff, pointing out that a lag would afford the chance for "development of a private government" within the industry which would later be difficult for the government to control.

President Johnson, in his opinion of the Traffic Safety Act, termed it "landmark legislation. For the first time in our history we can mount a truly comprehensive attack on the rising toll of death and destruction on the nation's highways."

Four years later, in 1970, Ralph Nader settled his subsequent suit against GM for invasion of privacy in an out-of-court settlement for $425,000 in damages. (The lawyers got one-third after expenses and Nader kept approximately $270,000.) He announced that he would pour the funds into further monitoring of General Motors' record on safety, pollution and consumer relations.

It was similar to a pledge he made at the hearings, where he said that all the royalties from *Unsafe At Any Speed* would go to the cause of auto safety. The pledge was quite a blow to GM's assertion that the book was merely profit-making sensationalism. Did this cause the corporate mirror-image that Nader accused GM executives of being blinded by to change? Apparently not. In April, 1971, James Roche issued a statement which said that although "America is the envy and the aspiration of the world . . . there are those who maintain our economic system is not the best, and ask is there not a better way. Some who question our society and its achievements are young. Some are well-intentioned. Some are sincere.

"But there are others. Their final objectives are not what they first profess. Their beliefs, their purposes, run contrary to the principles of the majority of our people. They question many of our institutions, including our economic system. They crusade for radical changes in our system of corporate ownership, changes so drastic that they would all but destroy free enterprise as we know it. Deliberately or not, they are also weakening our free competitive system.

". . . the dull cloud of pessimism and distrust that some have cast over free enterprise is impairing the ability of business to meet its basic economic responsibilities—not to mention its capacity to take on newer ones. This, as much as any other factor, makes it urgent that those of us who are in business, who have made business our career, who are justifiably proud of our profession, that we stand up and be counted. It is up to us to reaffirm our belief in free enterprise."

His speech was entitled "Critics Hit At Heart Of Free Enterprise," and was apparently an attack against Nader and others like him; an attempt to label the Naderisms in some way; to make the critics less than American.

In any event, Ralph Nader was not one to easily be pinned down, as GM should have learned years before. But then Ralph Nader appears to be a little bit more than most of us; more dedicated, more involved and more able to enjoy whatever he is doing.

The Auto Aftermath

The affair GM played with the detective story scenario was over, but Nader vs. GM was far from over. This was only the beginning. However, Nader realized that his single-handed, sporadic monitoring of the auto industry would be ineffective. Therefore, he decided to set up the Center For Auto Safety (CAS) which was to be funded by Consumers Union and to be independent of, but affiliated with, Nader. Lowell Dodge is director of the Center and his prime purpose is to keep a sharp eye on the National Highway Safety Bureau.

CAS is located on the eighth floor of a modern office building on 14th Street in Washington, D.C. Inside the small office, the activity reaches almost hectic proportions with people constantly talking, typing and the phone incessantly ringing. Most of the CAS workers are young, in their twenties or thirties, casually dressed, most with jeans and long hair. And they seem to fulfill very neatly the image of a stereotyped Nader's Raiders. Although only eight people are listed on the payroll, at least a dozen workers perform various office duties. Most of them work for next to nothing, since their organization is almost always broke. The money for the Center comes mainly from donations and book royalties.

Some of the personnel work for as low as $20 a week. And the lawyers receive only $90. But they survive by living in communal arrangements, giving up some luxuries, and not owning cars.

"It's amazing," said one of the staff members, "how much money a car can cost and how much you can save by not owning one." And to these people, it's worth the sacrifice. They feel they are accomplishing good things.

Liza, the top secretary in the office, gets a medium (on the CAS payscale) salary of maybe $50. Before joining the Nader operation she was a fashion buyer with a degree in Business Administration. But not enjoying her work very much and looking around for something better, she finally landed with CAS. Now she feels she's doing "something worthwhile."

The effectiveness of CAS can be measured by the proposals which they have helped introduce: child-seating regulations, the passive restraint bill (usually referred to as the air bag or cushion), and improved tire standards. Many other proposals are being written and researched.

One of the CAS's current projects is computerizing the 21,000 complaint letters which they have received since 1969, most of which have arrived in the last nine months. Most of the letters come from lawyers with questions on the viability of law-suits against auto manufacturers for damages incurred as a result of automobile accidents, or concerning manufacturing defects. CAS says they receive more complaints against VW's, Volvos, Opals, and Toyotas in the foreign car market; in the domestic market, Chevrolets, the most common American-made automobiles on the road, top the field by far.

Since Ralph Nader is the name most of the letter writers have become familiar with, the letters are often addressed to him. "Dear Mr. Nader," one complainant wrote, "In February of 1965, I purchased a 1964 model Chrysler New Yorker . . ." The letter went on to list the problems the owner had had with his new car—the windshield wiper was defective at the time of purchase;

the brakes on the front wheels had to be replaced twice during the first 10,000 miles of use; in less than 10,000 miles of use the power hose had to be replaced and the owner was informed by the dealer that the warranty did not cover the replacement. He also complained that the paint job was inferior," and "since this was a cash deal . . . any adjustment was difficult to get." He stated that he had written three letters of complaint to the Chrysler Corporation but had received no reply.

His letter ended rather wistfully, it seemed, "I have driven six Chrysler automobiles and until now have received good service from them."

That seemed to be a typical non-lawyer letter received at the center, in which the owner complained of everything from poor quality in workmanship to dangerous design hazards, citing genuine reasons for complaint and generally asking for help.

Those letters were probably a large influence on Tom Vacar, who once worked at the Center, when he decided to open the auto-complaint center. Vacar had already had a personal experience with a legitimate complaint against some auto repair shops, when in 1969 he took his 1963 Ford Galaxie to a large Ford dealer in Cleveland. Told that the repairs would cost $130, Vacar left his car. But when he picked it up the repair bill had jumped to exactly twice the estimated amount. And his cries of outrage did nothing to lower the $260 bill.

Afterwards, working for the Center for Auto Safety, Vacar realized that there were many people who had been similarly frustrated by repair shops, auto dealers and the auto manufacturers themselves. So after his summer with CAS, Vacar returned to Cleveland, where he set up his experimental center.

Financing was a problem and still is, but Nader contributed a total of $1,300 and Consumers Union gave the center two grants totaling $1,000. The United Auto Workers also gave $200.

Mr. Vacar's center has been very popular and surprisingly effective; so effective, in fact, that more centers are being planned elsewhere. One has been started in New York City by a consumer group, and the United

Auto Workers union have opened another in Cleveland. Bob Weissman, council President of the Cleveland council, says that UAW members are "doubly victimized." They are forced to work so fast on the assembly lines, Weissman says, that high quality work is impossible. And then they must purchase those same "shoddily made" cars, like everyone else.

Owners complain to the centers such as Vacar's, and the centers write letters, make phone calls and sometimes even visit the manufacturers' offices. Very often the centers win their points. Another feature of the centers is that they charge no fees—great for the consumers, but difficult for the financially troubled Vacar Center to handle. And the free and willing volunteer spirit of his college student assistants dwindled as the money dwindled. Even so, the center's work goes on.

"This center really works," Vacar said in a recent interview. "The consumer movement is powerless unless you get to the local level and solve complaints. And we have helped the consumer in eighty percent of the 400 complaints that we've handled."

Vacar also said that the center was not anti-business and asserted that he provided a stimulus to the free-enterprise system.

Another stimulus of sorts to the free-enterprise system was a "Lemon-Aid" book which came out of the Washington, D.C. Center for Auto Safety. Published by Grossman in the summer of 1971, *What to Do With Your Bad Car: An Action Manual for Lemon Owners* is a guidebook detailing how to avoid a lemon in the first place and what to do about it if you find yourself owning one. Ralph Nader, Lowell Dodge and Ralf Hotchkiss were the authors of the book, although Nader, of course, received most of the credit in the press due to his more familiar name.

Among the many ways suggested to "creatively seek out points of corporate vulnerability" is the protest letter. Nader suggests that carbon copies of a letter of complaint to a manufacturer should be mailed to the dealer, a lawyer, the President's Committee on Consumer Interests, the buyer's Senator and Congressman, the Federal Trade

Commission, the Center For Auto Safety, and a local newspaper or radio "action line," the National Automobile Dealers' Association and the state or local dealer-licensing authority. That probably will bring some action, but if not, the lemon-aid book goes on to further methods of achieving satisfying conclusion of the lemon ownership.

Most of the auto industry criticism emanated from CAS and the people who work there, rather than Nader himself. Nader, of course, is extremely busy with a wide variety of other consumer complaints. But Nader does still retain a large interest in the monitoring of the auto industry. Perhaps the safety defect in which he took the most personal and active interest after the Corvair case was another of the Nader vs. GM affairs—the incident of the defective engine mounts in the 1965–69 Chevrolets.

In January, 1971, Nader released a letter which he had written to Transportation Secretary John A. Volpe, in which he had asked Volpe to personally intervene in the investigation of the Chevrolet engine mounts. In the letter, which he released to the press, Nader said that he had received more than 300 complaints about the engine mount problem since September, 1970, and that GM had received about 1,500. Nader also claimed that GM had replaced, under their warranty guarantee, "some 100,000 engine mounts."

"You must act to halt the spread of this mechanical epidemic which may afflict as many as one in ten cars now on the nation's highways," Nader wrote to Volpe. And he also accused the National Highway Transportation Safety Administration (NHTSA), which is part of the Transportation Department, of having the most "callous disregard" for the safety of the Chevrolet owners involved.

In asking Volpe to intervene, Nader said that "under the pressure of your action, and complaints from thousands of owners, General Motors might also be awakened to their responsibility to repair the remaining defective Chevrolets at their own expense."

But if Volpe did respond to Nader's request, there was no immediately discernible action from the NHTSA. So

Nader continued his pressure for action by sending a letter to Douglas W. Toms, head of NHTSA, charging that the agency was guilty of "negligent inaction." He said that "time is of the essence" in investigating and correcting unsafe conditions in automobiles, but that the agency's investigations "frequently drag on for many months or even years." He further charged that the material on file was not accessible to him or his associates, that there was no way for the public to know when a defect investigation had begun. And why, he asked, didn't the agency force the auto maker to notify auto owners of safety defects?

Nader said his letter was only the beginning of his study of safety defects. He would continue to send letters directly to the head of NHTSA—which would also then be released to the press.

The main charge Nader hurled at Mr. Toms was that the agency just wasn't aggressive enough in their investigations and in forcing the companies to eliminate most safety defects in the design or early production stage. The letter also listed thirteen defects which Nader charged could affect "millions" of cars, and which have been the subject of numerous complaints directed to him from car owners.

Among these alleged defects: engine fires in Ford Capri 1971 models. In April of 1971, Ford had recalled the Pinto because of the possibility of fires due to fuel evaporative-emission-system defects. Nader said that two letters from Capri owners questioned whether or not the Capri also had this defect, enough to warrant an immediate investigation.

He also pointed out that the Chrysler Corporation might be in violation of federal standards for brake operation in their 1967–71 model cars. Reports from owners, he said, indicated that a number of models didn't brake correctly, and Nader felt an immediate investigation was in order.

There were eleven others, but Nader saved his strongest blast for those same Chevrolet engine mounts in the 1966 to '69 models. The agency's investigation of this purported defect should be expanded to include all the 1966–69 full-size Chevrolets and Camaros, and to speed up the action "before more tragedy ensues," Nader wrote. If the engine mount broke on these particular autos, the engines would lift, causing the accelerator to stick in the fully open position, and breaking the power brake lines. The driver would then have a speeding car with no braking power.

In October, General Motors denied the allegation. Edward Cole, President of GM, said there was no real danger with the model cars involved in the controversy, and that no recall should be made on approximately seven million cars. GM's statement came after a consumer bulletin had been issued by the government, warning owners of Chevrolet, Nova, Chevelle and Camaro models of the 1965–69 model years that they faced a "potential risk" in driving their cars.

Mr. Cole, at a news conference, said this was untrue. There was, he said, a possibility of engine mount failure, but this possibility was "not significant." He further stated that, "a person driving a car should be a skillful driver, and if he can't manage a car at under twenty-five miles per hour, he shouldn't be driving."

Mr. Cole's reference to the low speed was because of GM's assertion that only at a low speed was there a "safety risk" involved. Only a car accelerating rapidly from a slow speed or standing start caused enough thrust upon the engine to push it upwards (if the engine mounts broke) and cause the acceleration and braking problems.

"The condition takes place at very low speeds, where the car is completely controllable," Mr. Cole stated. "It's no different than having a flat tire or a blowout where you don't expect it."

But Mr. Cole's statement was contradicted by some owners. They said their cars had lurched forward so suddenly that they had hit another car or some object long before they could turn off the ignition and put the car in neutral.

General Motors was trying desperately not to have to recall the autos for replacing or repairing the motor mounts. It would be the most expensive recall in history. But the pressure by Nader for that recall was intense, and by December, 1971, GM had decided there was no other recourse.

Announcing that 6.7 million Chevrolet cars would be recalled to correct the engine mount problem, GM insisted that the problem was not a safety defect. "It is apparent that, as a result of the publicity that has been given to the engine mount issue, there is a great deal of misinformation and misunderstanding on the part of Chevrolet owners, which we are anxious to eliminate as soon as possible," GM said.

Motor mounts are rubber and metal sandwiches located between the automobile frame and the engine. Their purpose is to prevent the engine vibrations from passing into the rest of the car. And while it is true, as GM claimed, that the rubber part of the motor mount could not have the longevity that the metal parts have, there obviously was a design defect in these particular ones, if one considers the several thousand complaints received from owners concerning the problem, and if one considers that GM has already replaced 100,000 of them under warranty conditions.

But the case of the GM engine mounts was not over. In February, 1972, a 1.26 billion dollar class action lawsuit was filed against GM. The suit was filed by attorney Jeramiah Casselman, who represented three women owners of Chevrolets. It was charged that GM failed to make effective repairs on the 6.7 million Chevrolets recalled and accused GM of breach of warranty, fraud and misrepresentation. They also asked for one billion dollars in exemplary damages.

Poor GM? Some people would probably think so by now. But there are other past and future problems. In 1970, GM had reluctantly agreed to replace the defective front wheels on 50,000 trucks, after pressure from NHTSA. But 50,000 wasn't good enough for Ralph Nader. He was convinced that the front wheels on 200,000 of GM's 1960–65 model pickup trucks were defective due to a basic design failure. And after consulting with independent engineers and victims of crashes, he came up with what he considered enough proof to go to court. Part of his proof came from a Syracuse University metallurgist named Volker Weiss. Weiss said the failures could be traced to cracks in the metal which were caused by the manufacturing process.

In June, a Federal judge ordered the Department of Transportation to reconsider its settlement with General Motors concerning the defective front wheels. Under the compromise agreement reached between GM and the Transportation department, GM had agreed to recall only the 50,000 trucks for replacement of front wheels—trucks which had been outfitted with camper bodies and other special accessories.

And if the trucks weren't enough, there was more to come. In 1972, NHTSA and a Washington-based auto safety laboratory decided to run tests on 1971 Chevrolet Impalas and other GM cars, following reports that loose gravel and dirt could jam the automobiles' steering mechanisms while in motion.

And: In April, 1972, 130,000 Vegas were recalled by GM because of a possible fire hazard involving the fuel and exhaust systems. General Motors said that the recall was already underway before it learned of a letter written by Ralph Nader to NHTSA, complaining of the leisurely pace the agency was affecting in their investigation of the engine fire hazard. In his letter to the agency, Nader also said he had forwarded nine letters telling of similar fire hazards in the late model 1969–71 Ford LTDs. Other letters forwarded described fires in one Torino and one Cougar. In some cases the cars caught fire while parked in a driveway.

Nader said that the "painfully slow rate at which NHTSA pursues fire-related defect investigations is matched only by the agonizingly protracted deaths of victims of vehicle fires." His accusations grew out of an investigation which was four years old and which had twice been closed by the government, only to be reopened—the last time due to Nader's prodding. The original investigation concerned engine fires in some 1965 and 1966 GM cars and 1969–1971 LTDs.

And: The Senate Commerce Committee listened to sworn testimony that GM had bottled up evidence of a safety hazard in one aspect of the original Chevrolet

Corvair controversy—carbon monoxide fumes from defective heaters in Corvairs of the model years 1961 through 1969. These cars were equipped with direct-air heaters which had been allegedly causing leakage of carbon monoxide and other engine fumes into the passenger compartment.

The "bottled-up evidence" accusation came from Edward Wolfe, a Philadelphia attorney, who had made an out-of-court settlement for his client with GM for $125,000. His client had contended in a suit against GM that the carbon monoxide fumes from the defective Corvair heater had caused him permanent organic brain damage.

The $125,000 settlement contained a necessary condition however, Wolfe testified. The condition was that Wolfe had to turn over the incriminating evidence to the company, and include an amendment to the settlement which would attribute the carbon monoxide leakage to a cracked cylinder rather than to the heater's design. Mr. Wolfe also maintained that GM had known about the possible danger of the direct-air heater system from the beginning of the manufacturing process, and quoted from a 1961 Chevrolet Corvair shop manual to back up his contention:

"Because of the inherent characteristics of the heater, objectionable fumes may be taken into the passenger compartment and result in owner complaints . . . However, complaints of objectionable odors in the passenger compartment, whether the heater is on or off, should be traced immediately and promptly corrected."

At the time Mr. Wolfe testified before the Commerce Committee, a number of other damage suits were pending or had been settled. Class action suits in California and Ohio were asking damages for all Corvair owners in those states.

Poor GM? It hardly seems so.

But GM, although hardest hit, was not the only auto manufacturer to wear the mark of Nader. Ford, already smarting from similar Nader attacks, in January, 1972 was strongly urged by the Nader-associated Center for Auto Safety to recall approximately four million full-sized

Fords, Mercuries, Thunderbirds, and Continentals of model years 1964–69 for replacement of lower control arms. Ford insisted that the control-arm failure was due to driver misuse, but the Value Engineering Laboratory, a private testing agency, said that "the complete failures thus far examined show no evidence that they were primarily caused by driver abuse, such as striking curbings."

Nader did not restrict his probe into the auto industry to the United States, either. In 1972 at an eight-hour seminar in London, Ralph Nader blasted both the British Auto Association and the British auto manufacturers. And he didn't stop there. He hit the insurance industry, the press, and the Transportation Ministry, all of whom were accused of meek submission to auto interests.

And then along came his battle with the bug.

A 200-page report issued by the Center for Auto Safety, in September 1971, threatened to blow the Beetle right off the road. Titled, *The Volkswagen, An Assessment of Distinctive Hazards,* the report listed project editors as Lowell Dodge, Ralf Hotchkiss, Carl Nash, Stephen Oesch, and Bernard O'Meara. It also contained a foreword by Ralph Nader.

In the foreword, Nader called the Volkswagen "seriously unstable" with "collapse characteristics in a crash reminiscent of a Japanese lantern."

Nader also explained his reasons for picking on the beloved bug. "The justification for singling out VW's rests on several grounds: (a) since there are large numbers of them on American roads, their design defects are affecting many people: (b) there has been sufficient study of the VW to expose most of its safety problems, while similar defects have not been analyzed in less common cars; and (c) the VW is the leader of the subcompact field; it is almost solely responsible for both the wave of domestic compact cars around 1960 and the new series of subcompact U.S.-made cars . . . As the leader in its field, VW should assume an extra measure of responsibility for safe design."

The report recommended that VW institute an immediate 184-million dollar recall program to correct dangerous defects in the type I cars. The type I is the familiar Beetle.

The type II VW—which is the bus, camper or van model—the report alleged was "so unsafe that it should be removed from the roads entirely." Owners of the type IIs whose vehicles were to be removed should then, the report said, be refunded their money at current retail value, or be provided with free major insurance policies.

Volkswagen spokesmen dismissed the report. The Beetles "meet or exceed all safety standards," they said, and added that their cars are "providing millions of owners with safe, dependable and economical transportation."

Others also rushed to the defense of the Beetle, including *Road & Track* magazine. In an article by John Tomerlin titled "Ralph Nader Vs. Volkswagen" published in the April, 1972 issue, the following conclusion was reached: "In his foreword Ralph Nader speaks of an 'ethical imperative' on the part of Volkswagen to withdraw its cars for modifications. We believe we see a different imperative. In light of the total failure of the Nader Report to prove its charges . . . considering the enormous publicity the Report has received . . . and in view of the considerable damage the Report may have done to the Volkswagen company and owners of its products:

"*Road & Track* recommends that Ralph Nader observe the 'ethical imperative' to recall the VW Report and publicly retract its inaccuracies."

Among the "inaccuracies" of the Report, according to *Road & Track,* were "the use of partial test results and selected statistics", "the frequent failure to quote fully from its own sources, or to cite the conclusions of the Report to be "as irresponsible as it is unjustified." The article also said that *Road & Track*'s aim was not to criticize Nader personally.

In any event, that Report and the subsequent publicity of charges and counter-charges is not the end of the VW attack. *Small—On Safety, The Designed-In Dangers of the Volkswagen,* scheduled for publication by Grossman Publishers on August 14th, 1972, should bring the Volkswagen-Nader pot to a fine boil.

To be published along with the VW book is an updated

version of *Unsafe At Any Speed.* The updated version, according to Grossman, has "a new introduction of 30,000 words—that's about eighty pages. It updates things, brings out wonderful new stories about such things as the Corvair, GM's general suppression on safety devices, planning the passage of the Highway Safety Act, the actions and inactions of the National Highway Transportation Safety Bureau, and what safety standards still are needed."

Nader's criticism of the actions and inactions of NHTSA, which will be in the updated version, is nothing new, by any means. The ink was barely dry on the papers authorizing NHTSA before Nader started taking the agency to task. And he has been increasingly critical of the agency's actions ever since.

This was evident in his 1968 *Playboy* interview. After listing the progress which the agency brought about: safer windshields, collapsible steering columns, seat belts and safer dashboards, and the fact that the auto-safety issues are now "public issues and not the private domain of the auto manufacturers," Nader went on to say that "this is all good . . . [but] it isn't nearly enough."

More resources should be allocated to the fight for traffic safety, he said. "The fight doesn't end with the passage of a law; it just begins there. Without daily concrete support from the private sector, the law could be rendered a dead letter." Nader went on to recommend that the law be amended to provide penalties for noncompliance, either by fining the owner or by deregistering the car until it's repaired.

The absence of the "penalties for noncompliance" is Nader's biggest gripe against the Traffic Safety Law. He offers the reasonable argument that without penalties, there is no reason for auto manufacturers to do anything they don't want to. And they would have wanted to a lot less than they have, if Ralph Nader as the consumer advocate did not focus public attention on many problems concerning auto safety. For with the absence of a penalty clause in the law, public opinion, as Ralph Nader well knows, is the only effective force which can be used against the industry.

That effective force of public opinion will be, Nader hopes, his main weapon in his current fights—for the adoption of the air bag restraints in automobiles, for the industry's compliance to the standards of a "crash-worthy automobile," and in his fight with another giant—The American Automobile Association.

In July of 1971, Nader announced that he was opening an investigation of the thirteen million member AAA. Nader contended that AAA supported the "auto industry's disdain" for automobile safety and pollution. He claimed there was a "vast difference between the appearance of the AAA and the reality of its operations and policies—usually to the detriment of the AAA's membership."

The investigation was to be headed by Ron Landsman, a University of Michigan law student, who was to be assisted by students spending the summer digging into the politics and affairs of AAA. It was scheduled to find out who controls the association's policies, the influence of the members and "the potential of the auto clubs to make major contributions toward the health and safety of auto users."

The heretofore sacrosanct AAA has grown from about 1,000 members in 1902 to today's membership of about 13.5 million. It takes in close to one billion dollars a year in dues, premiums, commissions and other fees—"a revenue total that would rank it among the top 120 or 130 industrial concerns in the nation, were AAA a company rather than a nonprofit organization," said the *Wall Street Journal.*

The main criticism against the AAA was their almost solid support of the use of federal and state gas taxes for roadbuilding—*only.* Critics say that this hinders efforts to alleviate air pollution and the development of mass transit as an alternative to the automobile.

"Partly because of AAA's influence, twenty-eight states have gas funds that can legally be spent only on highways, and many other states adhere in practice to the same rule," the *Wall Street Journal* continued.

In retaliation against the Nader-inspired investigation, the head of the AAA accused Nader of hurting the safety effort. William Bachman, President of AAA, said that

Ralph Nader "is doing the cause of safety a dangerous disservice." He charged that Nader's Raiders were a "small, organized [minority] who, however, command attention far beyond their size in numbers." And harping on the familiar theme, Mr. Bachman continued: "I am afraid that the single-minded focus on cars promoted by Mr. Nader and taken up by his sycophants, is taking the public's eye off the real culprits—the driver and the highway."

Lest anyone think for an instant that this is true, listen to what Nader has said in various ways since he became involved in the issue of safe cars. "Let's have good drivers—but above all, let's have good cars for them to drive."

Concerning the issue of a safer automobile, the added cost of such cars has risen repeatedly. In March, 1972, a report prepared for the White House Office of Science and Technology warned that government-proposed safety and pollution regulations may in some cases become too expensive, and would add almost $900 to the cost of an automobile.

Nader, of course, felt the report to be less than accurate. He said it was "another effort to intimidate the Federal regulatory agencies responsible for regulating motor vehicle air pollution and safety." And that it "uses a mass of erratic statistics to prove that air pollution and safety regulations are not worth the cost to the consumer, but disregards the excessive industry profit margins and outrageous costs of unneeded and unwanted 'standard equipment' installed on cars."

Among the increased costs purported by the report were the air bag system—a gas-inflated cushion of woven nylon that is folded and hidden inside the instrument panel. Nader has, even as early as 1966, espoused the use of passive restraints in automobiles, and in *Unsafe At Any Speed,* he indicated that air bags might be just the right answer to the restraint problem.

Because of Nader and the Center for Auto Safety's interest and lobbying on behalf of such a passive restraint system, the Transportation Department issued the so-called "air bag rule" on May 7, 1970. This proposal was to later become the controversial 1971 Standard 208. The Standard 208 to the auto industry meant that they would have to install air bags in their 1974-model cars. But the auto makers cried foul, and asked for reconsideration of the order by the Transportation Department, and decided to challenge it in the courts.

Nader, realizing that the auto industry might get what they wanted, urged the Transportation Secretary to hold fast to the original deadline. In a public letter to Volpe, Nader noted that he, Volpe, had supported the air bag idea "to the point of high personal identification with its life-saving value."

Continuing with his letter, Nader wrote: "You have large suppliers of this feature showing how practical the feature is and how capable they are in tooling up for production. You have a solid unanimity of your National Highway Traffic Safety Administration staff and director for no further postponement." Nader said that nothing should postpone the deadline—"not technical capability, production capability, or any other obstacle, except the corporate avarice for maximizing profits—stands in the way of your decision to uphold the present deadline."

The courts have not yet ruled, and the issue is still up in the air. But if the government is at all influenced by a study which was ordered to look into the issue, the balance seems to be tipping toward the auto companies' viewpoint.

In a study entitled "Cumulative Regulatory Effects on the Cost of Automobile Transportation," or RECAT, the air bag got deflated.

"The cost of the air-bag system," the study said, "is substantially greater than that of the harness system, although future production experience can be expected to reduce this differential. The regulation (requiring the installation of the air bag or some other passive restraint, as amended, starting with the 1976 models) thus effectively will require the willing harness user to pay more for passive restraints that may not afford him more protection."

Nader won't take this lying down, of course, nor will the Center for Auto Safety, but if the government decides to go along with the auto industry's interests, there is little Nader can do about it, except to try once again to get public opinion to act as an effective weapon.

Nader's Raiders

They fit somewhere between the very square and the very radical. More often than not they are from Ivy League schools. They are almost always white and only incidentally female. (Blacks have not flocked to Nader in any number. Some don't like the pay. Others would rather work on black problems.) There are more lawyers and law students among them than any other group, though medical, engineering, economics and liberal arts students have been among their number in the past. And they are young, ranging in age from their early twenties to their early thirties. Who are they? They are Nader's Raiders, his young professional and student task force that he has spent after a variety of business and governmental ills.

The first group of Nader's Raiders came to Washington in the summer of 1968. Nader's influence on the auto issue was at its zenith but he felt there were many other things to be tackled, and his own resources—financial and physical were limited.

Nader chose as the summer's project an investigation

of the Federal Trade Commission, and he picked a handful of Ivy Leaguers to do the scouting. Robert Fellmeth, now a senior Raider, a co-author of the FTC report, the editor of the ICC report and now directing the massive Nader study on Congress, attended Stanford and Harvard Law. Edward Cox, Tricia Nixon's husband, had attended Princeton and Harvard Law. William Howard Taft IV, a great-grandson of President William Howard Taft, had gone to Yale and Harvard Law. Judy Areen, who had gone to Cornell and Yale Law, was the daughter of the head of Chrysler's sales financing company. The others on the project were Andrew Egendorf (MIT-Harvard Law), Peter Bradford (Yale-Yale Law), and John Schulz, who Nader named as the project's director, had gone to Princeton and Yale Law.

Nader outlined an approach to the investigation of the FTC and then left the group pretty much to its own devices. A preliminary draft of the report was released in the fall of 1968 and an edited version of the report appeared in 1969.

The Raiders found a strong bias toward business, toward partisan consideration and toward cronyism—FTC lawyers seemed to come out of the Southern law schools rather than Eastern schools, a fact the Raiders thought was reinforced by the largely Southern hierarchy of the FTC. In summary, the Raiders found what everyone in Washington had known all along—that the FTC was ineffective.

Richard Nixon got the American Bar Association to study the FTC and it released its report in September of 1969. The results, though tempered with bureaucratic prose, said the same thing—the FTC was not doing its job. Subsequently, the chairman of the report committee, Miles Kirkpatrick, became chairman of the FTC and committee counsel Robert Pitofsky became head of the FTC's newly formed consumer protection arm.

It was after an FTC hearing in November of 1968, at which the Raiders were confronted by then FTC Chairman Paul Rand Dixon, that they were dubbed by a newspaper reporter, "Nader's Raiders."

The Raiders' methodology was one that they were to

use on almost all subsequent reports: Interview those at the agency or the company being studied—at least insofar as the higher-ups will make themselves available for such interviews; assemble as much data as is public (even if it means having to sue for release of records, in the case of a government agency, under the Freedom of Information Act), and read everything already available in the area.

The results of the study drew great coverage. The study group was elated. However, the shouting was not over what they had compiled but over the fact that Ralph Nader had done it again. He had smelled a rat, and he had gotten the facts together to back up his suspicions.

In the fall of 1968, Nader made the first step toward full-time propagation of his work. With the aid of various foundation grants he established the Center for the Study of Responsive Law, which in three years has become the backbone of the Nader organization.

Named as trustees of the Center were Nader's sister, Laura, Edmund Shaker, a Nader relative and Canadian barrister and solicitor, and two professors from the University of Michigan, Layman Allen and Paul W. Gikas. The Center has tax-exempt status since it is a non-profit educational organization. Nader himself is managing trustee, which means that he effectively martials and directs the Center's activities. The Center's associates receive from $10,000–$15,000 annually in salary. All could make a great deal more on the outside. The first five center members were John Esposito, James Turner, Reuben Robertson III, Gary Sellers and Harrison Wellford, who was the center's first executive director.

Esposito, thirty-two, and a graduate of Harvard Law School, wrote the Nader Study Group Report on air pollution called *Vanishing Air*. Turner, a graduate of Ohio State University Law School, wrote one of the better-selling Nader Study Group Reports, *The Chemical Feast,* an investigation of the FDA. He is no longer associated with Nader. He has in recent months worked with another Washington consumer advocate, John Banzaf, who teaches at George Washington University Law School, and heads up ASH, Action on Smoking and

Health. Turner and Nader disagreed about how one best went about raising consumer consciousness. "I talked it over with Ralph," Turner told William Greider of the Washington Post, "and there were definitely some differences about how to go about it, so we sort of agreed 'you try your way, I'll try mine and we'll see which one works.' " Reuben Robertson III, thirty, a Yale Law school graduate who worked for Covington and Burling, one of the largest political lobbyist firms in Washington, is now head of a consumer advisory group to the Civil Aeronautics Board. Gary Sellers, thirty-seven, the Center's legal counsel and a graduate of Michigan State Law School, spent four years working in the Bureau of the Budget. And Harrison Wellford, thirty-two, a political scientist from Harvard who was the first executive director of the Center, asked to relinquish that position so that he might spend more time researching. He is the author of the Nader study on the Department of Agriculture called *Sowing The Wind.*

The second executive director of the Center, Theodore Jacobs, thirty-seven, is effectively Nader's top lieutenant. Like Nader, he attended Princeton and Harvard Law School. Nadar grabbed Jacobs from a Wall Street law firm by way of the National Commission on Product Safety. Nader goaded Jacobs until he finally packed his bags and headed south to the Potomac. There are those who doubt Jacobs' true motives. Some claim he waited until Nader was established before signing on. Others think he may be aiming Nader for a career in politics.

The Center's $250,000 annual budget is primarily met by foundation money, including the Carnegie Foundation, the Stern Family Fund, and even by muffler king, Gordon (Midas) Sherman. In 1969 the Center received about $170,000 in contributions and this doubled in 1970.

The summer of 1969 saw some 100 Raiders deployed all over Washington. The most tangible results were three books: Fellmeth's *The Interstate Commerce Omission,* Turner's *The Chemical Feast* and Esposito's *Vanishing Air.* The enthusiasm with which those efforts were met caused Nader to redouble his efforts and pick some 200

Raiders (out of some 3,500 who applied) and disperse then on a plethora of projects for summer, 1970.

Among those projects: First National City Bank, DuPont in Delaware, think tanks, General Motors, supermarkets, food companies, paper and pulp industries in Maine, antitrust, the Bureau of Reclamation, the Forest Service, the National Institute of Mental Health, Connecticut's consumer and insurance departments, the quality of health care in hospitals, the pollution of Georgia's Savannah River, the use of land and water in California.

Getting to be a Nader's Raider is tougher than getting into most of the Ivy League colleges that the Raiders come from. About one in twenty who apply are chosen. The pay is poor ($200 to $1,500 for the summer) and if a Raider really doesn't need it he's expected to forego it.

The Center for the Study of Responsive Law, which houses the senior Raiders and serves as a watering post for the summer Raiders, is just off Dupont Circle in Northwest Washington.

The entrance to the Center is a nondescript door squeezed between two buildings. You have to climb a flight of narrow stairs to arrive at the Center's door. There's no need to knock for the door is always open, but in case you're still unsure of where you are, there's a hand-printed cardboard sign on the door which says in even lettering: Center for the S udy of Responsive Law. The main reception room is reminiscent of an old doctor's office, comfortable and commodious, but not showy, very much in character with the man who founded the Center. To be sure the digs of the Center are no plastic wonderland. Three large old scratched oak desks are piled high with papers and pamphlets such as the *Brief on Aviation Consumer Project,* prepared by Nader's Aviation Consumer Action Project. But it's not only the desks that bear the physical evidence of Nader activism. It's the window ledges, the file cabinets, even the corners of the room, all of which house the fruits of the labors of Nader's various groups.

The main focus of the room, however, is a huge mailbox. Nader receives most of his mail at the Center. Quite a bit is left for him to open personally. He reads most of it in his $80-a-month boarding house room or at the various small offices he has tucked around Washington, including an anonymous one in the National Press Building. Mail which is not personally addressed is slotted in the various project boxes.

The overall atmosphere of the Nader nerve center is pleasant. The mail room has lots of light, especially reflecting on the office's bright yellow mailbox. Environmental posters deck the walls. A row of colorful ties, made by one of the office staff and on sale for $5 each, adds a rather different note to the office.

One expects lots of long-haired college students in eccentric dress manning the desks and phones. Instead the secretaries are in their thirties and forties and the senior Raiders dress neatly if conservatively, suit coats thrown over the back of their chairs, ready for formal action at a moment's notice.

The atmosphere is busy but relaxed. One of the secretaries said, however, that she sometimes feels tired by 10 a.m. due to the incessant ringing of the phones. The secretaries have plenty of typing to do and have to cope with the mail as well as visitors. When someone needs a document or a Nader report or memo, the secretaries have to dig them out, a seemingly impossible task in the paper blizzard that covers the room.

The casual air of the office extends to the activities of those who work there. Lunch hours are flexible; there is time to take care of personal affairs, if necessary, during business hours. The prevailing philosophy appears to be, as long as you get your work done—and the all-important phones are manned by someone—then your work habits are your own business.

The office is not without its touches of humor. *Mad* magazine's takeoff on the contents of Ralph Nader's wallet is pinned on one wall. Next to that are title suggestions for Harrison Wellford's book on the Department of Agriculture: "Unsafe at any Feed" and "Cast your Fate to the Wind."

Theo Page is one of the younger women in the office. She is cheerful, helpful and bright. Originally from New York, she came to D.C. to teach and volunteered her services part-time in 1970. Soon it became more important for her to work as a Raider than teach, so she quit in order to work full-time at the Center. Her official capacity is receptionist-secretary, but in truth she said her title would more appropriately be traffic-conductor. Although putting in a full week's work, she receives wages for part-time hours only, volunteering the rest. Most of those not on the payroll are mothers who were secretaries once. "They seek something important and more challenging to do than being a secretary again," said Theo. "They don't need the money. So this work fills the need." Because of an announcement requesting volunteer services published in the American Association of Retired People's Newsletter last year, many of the volunteers are now older people. The response was large, beyond what was expected. Many of them retain excellent secretarial and mathematical skills, while others lick envelopes. They became so involved in consumerism that a group has been formed—the Group for Retired Professionals—to fight the fare hike for elderly people from half-fare to full in D.C. And of course there are the university students. For distinct projects the Center writes letters to universities and friendly professors asking for people who can fulfill certain functions; for more general work they accept local students. There is an overabundance of volunteers who fall into this general category. Theo refers them to other groups and hopes they can be used there.

Theo Page feels she is at last "doing something about our problems." The twenty or so people she works with are pleasant, college-educated, and dedicated folk. The fact that her wages are minimal doesn't daunt her.

As for contact with "famous people," Ralph Nader is about the only one who comes directly to the office. Most people phone or write. There are a lot of visits from press people; however, if it's to catch a candid snapshot of Nader they are out of luck, for he is in and out so sporadically and quickly that it's hard to catch him. His intense speaking schedule leaves little time to hang around—he delivers roughly eight speeches a week. A friend of Theo's working in another office said that a hush falls over the room whenever Nader walks in. She sees him as "a true inspiration . . . the driving force behind the entire operation . . . very, very nice . . . and an optimistic man . . . he clarifies the air when he walks in . . . very charismatic." He's been known to say that he works better under pressure and the more there is to do the better he likes it.

The rest of the office is composed of the respective offices of the senior Raiders, decent-sized but so filled with papers and jammed bookshelves that they appear cluttered and smaller than they actually are. There are three other room areas, one really quite large, with desks and bookshelves. On one young man's desk was a radio with rock music playing softly from it. One office had a hugh yellow op-art painting on the wall. These rooms were a bit more organized, except for occasional picket signs sticking up like cardboard trees with captions such as: "A.C.A.P.—Aviation Consumer Action Project" or "IATA: The End is Near" or "How Fare are Fares?: End Secret Price Fixing by Airlines Now." The bookshelves are stacked with technical material and journals such as *Congressional Digests, Office of Education* and *HUD Reports, Code of Federal Regulations* books, *Internal Revenue Code* books, *Who's Who in America, Standard and Poor's Register of Corporations, Directors,* and *Executives,* and boxes of Nader books in a tiny storage room.

Despite the lack of closed doors, phones ringing, and the constant stream of people, the office was generally peaceful and large enough to find a library-quiet corner.

There is never a dull moment at the Center. One day a very distraught, thin, blond woman in her late thirties came in coatless on a cold, March day saying "Am I crazy or what? I feel like I'm surrounded by Martians." Theo kept trying to find out what her problem was but the woman rambled on about how "they're trying to infiltrate . . ." and ran around the office holding her head, on the verge of tears. Ted Jacobs then came out of his office to leavc for an appointment. She addressed him, asking him if she were going mad. Jacobs, who had never seen her before, tried to get something coherent from her, finally gave up and maneuvered her to the doorway, closing the door on her. She left muttering down the stairs. The office was visibly upset by this event, although one secretary said that they frequently get crazy people in the office, or more often desperate people calling in claiming that "Ralph Nader is the only one who can help me. He's my last hope." They try to do what they can but they are usually dealing with an irrational element and can't do much.

The Congress project is the biggest Nader undertaking to date. In comparison to the others it will be on a huge scale and everyone is quite excited about it. It is the lack of any authoritarian atmosphere that creates casual feeling that permits people to be so cordial and pleasant. It seems everyone knows their job and just does it.

Harrison Wellford, the Harvard-trained political scientist, is the only one of the five original senior Nader's Raiders fellows at the Center who was not a lawyer. Wellford's main concern has been the Department of Agriculture, Federal Meat Inspection, food wholesomeness, and the misuses of pesticides. The 489-page report which he wrote (he also headed the task force which gathered the research) is due out sometime in 1972. Its title is *Sowing the Wind: Food Safety and the Chemical Harvest.* Wellford continues to monitor the agencies he wrote about in *Sowing the Wind,* as well as editing *The Consumer Protection Report,* a newsletter for both food inspectors and the general consumer.

Wellford's small office at the Center is piled from floor to ceiling with papers and reports. Unlike Nader he's a family man with a wife and child, and as such has to temper his zeal with the attendant responsibilities of father and husband. Nader's Raiders are always on call, but hearing from Ralph Nader at 1 a.m. over an extended period of nights is enough to light the fuse of even the most long-tempered wife.

When we talked with Wellford he seemed a bit harried. He had to testify in front of a Congressional subcommittee that afternoon and his phone rang constantly.

Q: How did you get involved with this? How long have you been working for the Center?

A: I was the first executive director of the Center. We founded it in July 1969. Before that I was teaching government courses at Harvard, been involved in the civil rights movement in the South off and on. My wife and I taught at a black college in the South and I spent a lot of time traveling in the deep South, mainly looking into hunger and the food delivery programs. I wrote a couple of pieces on that and became interested in the larger policy question of how our system of federal subsidies in agriculture that allowed this kind of human misery to exist. There seemed to be a vast amount of contrast between a man like Senator Eastland in Mississippi and the poverty of the black people living around his plantation. It was obvious to anyone who was down there. The question was how this kind of disparity came to be, and particularly the history behind the subsidy of cotton agriculture and the lack of support for the people driven off the farm. At first I was just concerned with how effective our programs were—food stamp program, etc. But as I got deeper into it I became concerned with how the whole system started in the beginning, which meant I had to come to Washington to study it first-hand.

I first worked with Ralph in 1966 when I was at Harvard Law School. That was when the GM issue was hot. He needed some research assistants so I and John Esposito came down with three other people. I worked on foreign aid, the delivery of surplus food to developing countries. After I got here my interest broadened enormously. I am now concerned with mainly environmental problems, safety problems, and broadening citizen participation in government decision making.

Q: How did you first become involved with Ralph Nader?

A: I read an article, the first about Ralph as a phenomenon, in the spring of '66 in the *New Republic*. That made me know who he was. It was a professor at the Yale Law School who put us together. After I worked for him that summer we kept in touch. Ralph experimented for a number of summers with the three-month task forces but there was no staying power with that system. We talked about how to give permanence to our work and the Center developed from that, with a grant from Carnegie to help us out. We started with five and have grown a great deal.

Q: How do you support yourself now?

A: Mainly through public support. Everybody has an issue which they are concerned about and willing to send us money for. Initially we needed foundation support, and still use it but aren't dependent on it now. The publications contribute marginally. In some cases we spent about as much as we'll ever get back just to publish the books.

Q: You've been campaigning against the use of nitrites and nitrates in food. Can you tell us more about that?

A: There's an example of what we *do* feel is important. We have just filed a petition asking for the ban of sodium nitrate in baby food and bacon and hot dogs within six months unless evidence can show that its use is necessary in the prevention of botulism. When sodium nitrate combines with secondary and tertiary amines, nitrosamines are formed, which are highly carcinogenic substances. There is no debate about it. It seems an obvious cautionary step to decrease the use of nitrate. We have a number of companies now producing a nitrate-free hot dog which shows that the technology does exist for manufacturing these foods without its use. Norway has banned its use effective November, 1972, unless it is proven necessary.

Q: Did you have anything to do with the Wholesome Meat Act of 1967?

A: That was before my time, though Ralph was quite active in it. I used it as an example of consumer activism in the book *Sowing the Wind*. There's no question that the bill as a whole was a success—the amount of marginal plants producing bad meat has decreased, the number of plants under federal inspection jurisdiction has increased, the standards under which meat is manufactured as a whole have gone up, but there are a number of serious problems still.

In the first place, there was a tremendous delay in its implementation, which was not warranted. Second, there is a question as to whether or not the state programs are in fact equivalent to federal programs. We have a lot of evidence that their standards are not as high. We testified on that this week, in fact.

The biggest problem with meat inspection is not actually sanitation but the chemical contamination of meat. This bill doesn't really address that issue at all, so we are working and monitoring that issue constantly. This will be a future focus.

Q: Do people consider you a fanatic?

A: Not really, because the issues we are involved with are pretty well grounded in research supported by established scientists. My response to our detraction is to have them read what we've put out and *then* form their conclusions. If there's solid evidence that amounts of a suspicious chemical are going into a food and there are ways of eliminating it without creating additional hazards, that makes sense. These decisions, more often than not, are political as well as scientific. We try to make sure that all the facts are there to be considered. This is a classic Madisonian approach. There's nothing the least bit radical about our approach.

Q: How do you like working with Nader?

A: Well, if I didn't have a positive answer to that question I wouldn't be here. Here I have as much responsibility and independence at a young age as I could have anywhere else. Ralph is a great source of advice, but basically he lets you go your own way and sink or swim. I like being able to set my own priorities, which is what he lets me do.

Also I like the variety of the work—I testified three times in the last five days, I'm involved in a book, I've just gotten back from investigating a company town down South—very multi-dimensional. I feel too that we are beginning to establish the permanent institution we envisioned in the first place, so it really is worth my while to be here.

I wish we had more money to have a more efficient office system. We need more secretaries and more clerical help. We get several hundred letters a week and it's very difficult for me to answer all of them. We have a very lean operation. I'm convinced that nobody gets as much output from people, though, as we do. We're small but very productive.

Q: Do you think that's the result of the dedication of people who feel they are really doing something?

A: Yes. I think also Ralph's example is pretty terrifying. I mean the guy works far more than anyone else here could. He doesn't have the obligations that some of us have, such as family, it's true. Nevertheless his dedication sets a standard that no one else can match. If you have a competitive instinct yourself and measure yourself, you'll never be complacent because you'll never match it. It's that kind of symbolism, if you will, that keeps everyone on their toes. You know, too, that Ralph supports the operation from his speaking arrangements. I've been on the speaking circuit a few times myself and I know what a grueling experience that can be. So if I'm slacking off a bit and I remember that Ralph is out in Dubuque, Iowa, someplace making a speech in the middle of the night, I feel guilty. It's that kind of drive that energizes the operation. We do have a fairly competitive system here; we're all aware of what the other people are doing and want to measure up. You could get away with doing a shoddy job for awhile but your own conscience would tell you to shape up, or other people would become aware of the fact that you weren't shaping up and this would set you back on your toes.

Q: How long do you feel Ralph Nader can keep up this frantic pace? If he should leave, would the Center carry on or would some of the incentive be gone?

A: Oh, people would carry on anyway. We have a lot of very good people here; their motivation is very high. We'd go on, although whether the public would be as interested is hard to say. There isn't anyone else here with Ralph's charisma—he has a very special magnetism that comes across.

Q: What about the Nader Mystique? Are you affected by that?

A: I've known Ralph for a long time now. I think Nader has special qualities that no one else I know has to the same degree—I'm convinced of that. His life to some degree is simplified—for example, he's not involved with raising a kid like I am, so that he doesn't feel a conflict between work and family. For example, if I felt my job were interfering with the raising of my daughter Susannah I would have to do something about it. He is sometimes insensitive to these kinds of needs, but once they are explained to him I've found him to be totally understanding.

Q: You mean you may have to stop him to remind him that for one reason or another you can't go at the pace he's going?

A: Sure, absolutely.

Q: Do you feel the organization is becoming too bureaucratic?

A: There are clearly a number of problems. There is a media overload as well as an influx of information and letters that our clerical help has difficulty handling. Letters often don't get answered for a long time; we can't address every problem that comes in; we are sometimes so busy that we become insensitive to problems even with our staff—not because we're insensitive but rather a function of the pressure here. Once you have a demand you feel compelled to meet it. This is a demanding situation and some people come here and are not prepared for it. Personally I have no complaints—I don't like a lot of supervision. When I need Ralph, he's there.

Q: Do you notice any personality changes since he's become a media figure?

A: I think anyone's personality changes in relation to the amount of pressure he takes on. I have become less approachable because of the tremendous amount of work I have now. It isn't through a lack of desire but rather through a lack of time—time is extremely short. We could spend all of our time talking to people with problems.

Q: But on a more personal level concerning Ralph Nader.

A: No, I don't see any basic change. I think the amount of pressure on him has increased, which in turn affects the amount of time he can spend with people as well, reduces his own personal resources for reacting to people's personal problems—at least this is my reaction when I'm extended to the limit. But I don't see any basic changes in him at all.

Q: Do you start your own projects now or still get ideas from Ralph?

A: Most of the time they come from me or my associates. Sometimes he starts projects, but I'm involved in some things he didn't even know about when they began.

Besides the great-grandson of a President and the son-in-law of another, there have been other well-known Raiders. Ken Dryden, the All-Star goalie for the Montreal Canadians, a graduate of Cornell University and a law student at Canada's McGill University, spent the 1971 off-season working in Washington as a Nader's Raider.

Claire Townsend, now a Princeton undergraduate, spent the summer of 1970 along with a handful of her classmates from the exclusive Miss Porter's school in Farmington, Connecticut, (Jacqueline Kennedy Onassis is an alumna) and headed a task force on Nursing Homes and care for the aged which resulted in *Old Age: The*

Last Segregation. The girls, mostly seventeen and eighteen, were the youngest Nader group yet. Claire's father is Robert Townsend, the former head of Avis who wrote the best selling book called *Up the Organization.* Townsend bought the girls a Washington town house so that they could spend the summer in Washington preparing the report. He also made a contribution of $150,000 to further Nader's efforts. The only stipulation: that Nader not tell him what he did with the money.

As of January 1972, various Nader study groups had released the following reports:

The Nader Report on the Federal Trade Commission
Robert Fellmeth, Project Director. Published by Grove Press, in both cloth ($6.95) and paperback ($1.95) editions.

The Interstate Commerce Omission
Robert Fellmeth, Project Director. Published 1970 by Grossman Publishers, in both cloth ($8.95) and paperback ($1.45) editions.

Vanishing Air
Nader Task Force Report on Air Pollution. John C. Esposito, Editor. Published 1970 by Grossman Publishers, in both cloth ($6.95) and paperback ($.95) editions.

The Chemical Feast
Nader Task Force Report on the Food & Drug Administration. James S. Turner, Editor. Published 1970 by Grossman Publishers, in both cloth ($6.95) and paperback ($1.45) editions.

One Life—One Physician: An Inquiry into the Medical Profession's Performance in Self-Regulation.
Robert S. McCleery, M.D., Editor. Published 1970 by Public Affairs Press, in cloth ($5.00) edition. 167 pages.

Old Age: The Last Segregation
Nader Task Force Report on Nursing Homes. Claire Townsend, Project Director. Published 1971 by Grossman Publishers, in cloth ($6.50) edition, and in paperback ($1.95) edition by Bantam Books, 1971.

The Water Lords
Nader Task Force Report on the Savannah River.

James Fallows, Editor. Published 1971 by Grossman Publishers, in cloth ($7.95) and in paperback ($1.95) by Bantam Books, 1971.

Water Wasteland

Nader Task Force Report on Water Pollution. David Zwick, Editor. Published 1971 by Grossman Publishers, in cloth ($7.95) edition.

The Closed Enterprise System

Nader Task Force Report on Antitrust Enforcement. Mark J. Green, Editor. 1971. Two-volume preliminary draft copies available. $27.50. 1154 pages.*

Citibank

Nader Task Force Report on First National City Bank. David Leinsdorf, Editor. 1971. Preliminary draft copies available. $15.00. 547 pages.*

Sowing the Wind: Meat, Pesticides and the Public Interest.

Harrison Wellford, Editor. Published 1972 by Grossman Publishers.

Power and Land in California

Nader Task Force Report on Land Use in California. Robert Fellmeth, Editor. 1971. Two-volume preliminary draft copies available. $30.00. 1200 pages.*

Tractor Safety Report

By James Williams, as reprinted in the September 17, 1969 *Congressional Record.* $2.00*

Crash Safety in General Aviation Aircraft

James Bruce and John Draper, Editors. Preliminary draft copies available. $5.00. 98 pages.*

Damming The West

Nader Task Force Report on Bureau of Reclamation. Richard L. Berkman, Kip Viscusi, Editors. 1971. Preliminary draft copies available. $10.00. 259 pages.*

The Company State: Dupont In Delaware

Nader Task Force Report on Corporate Responsibility. James Phelan and Robert Pozen, Editors. 1971. Two-volume preliminary draft copies available. $25.00. 850 pages.*

*Available in Xeroxed manuscript from the Center for Study of Responsive Law.

The Workers: Portraits of Nine American Job Holders.
Kenneth Lasson, Editor. 1971, cloth ($5.95) edition, Grossman Publishers.

What To Do With Your Bad Car: An Action Manual for Lemon Owners.
Ralph Nader, Lowell Dodge, and Ralf Hotchkiss. Published by Grossman Publishers, in cloth edition ($3.95) and in paperback ($1.50) edition by Bantam Books.

Action For a Change: A Manual for Organizing Student Public Interest Research Groups.
Ralph Nader, Donald Ross, Brent English and Joe Highland. Available in book stores $1.35. Published by Grossman Publishers.

Scheduled for publication in 1972 were Wellford's *Sowing The Wind, The Closed Enterprise System* (the antitrust report), *Whistleblowing* (culled from the Conference on Professional Responsibility that Nader held in 1971), *Small of Safety* (a report on the VW, another Nader pet target), *The Company State* (DuPont influence in Delaware), *The Monopoly Makers* (anti-trust and the regulatory agencies), *Corporate Power In America,* and *Damming The West* (a look at the U.S. Bureau of Reclamation).

A revised edition of *Unsafe At Any Speed* including some 30,000 new words is also due from Richard Grossman, Nader's original publisher who released *Unsafe* and all the subsequent Nader's Raider's reports. Nader respects loyalty and gives it in turn. Grossman went out on a limb to publish *Unsafe* and Nader, though any one of a number of publishers would be glad to handle publication of his reports, has stuck with the small and personalized attention that the Grossman operation affords.

Tom Stewart, a Grossman editor, says that in general the reports need little rewriting but lots of cutting. After pruning one third of the manuscript, *Water Wasteland* was still a 512-page book. *The Interstate Commerce Omission,* which is about 450 pages, has a note in it saying you can write in and get supplementary data which length forced the study group to leave out. *Politics or Land* (on land use in California), and *The Closed Enterprise System* were both 1,200 pages in manuscript, much too long for the average reader to wade through.

Stewart adds: "Sometimes, if I feel the discussion has gotten too complicated I will approach the writer and say just that and work with him on it. Sometimes there is an unnecessary number of examples offered. I let the authors determine which facts are the necessary ones.

"The source of these problems is that the reports are written in such great haste that they aren't as well-digested as they ought to be. Many times the author will go back and read something written a couple of months ago and realize that half the stuff included isn't necessary to make his point. It's useful information to have for other purposes but for this kind of communication it isn't necessary."

Most of the books, says Stewart, sell 5,000–10,000 in hardcover, a respectable figure. The paperback sales vary, *The Chemical Feast* at 175,000 has done better than say *The Interstate Commerce Omission* at 75,000. Stewart's boss, Richard Grossman, recently changed distribution companies for the paperback editions. He says the old distributor "didn't have a strong enough distribution setup to circulate the books in large enough quantities at cheap enough prices to reach the most people, and that's our objective."

Grossman smiles when asked if he gets tons of manuscript on consumer problems: "By the fistful . . . but don't overhonor us. We're neither more nor less daring than others."

What's in the works? Well, things will probably come a bit slower. Nader cut the number of Raiders from 200 in the summer of 1970 to fifty in 1971. The larger number meant more unsupervised Raiders, and those close to the projects say that unfortunately every prospect did not turn out to be a mini-Nader, so the reduction to fifty was a step toward quality control, although Nader and his top lieutenants would probably not concede as much.

Of the projects announced for summer 1970 the following have not been published, either in draft form by the Center or by Grossman: a project on think tanks such as Hudson Institute and the Rand Corporation, supermarkets, food companies (except as embodied in Wellford's book), paper and pulp industries in Maine, the Forest Service, the National Institute of Mental Health, the National Academy of Science, COMSAT, and the State of Connecticut's consumer and insurance departments (a preliminary report was prepared and it caused quite a stir, however it is not listed in the Center's catalogue of publications.) A report on the American Automobile Association and just how "consumer-oriented" it is, is also in the offing. Other possible reports: property tax, the influence of lobby law firms like Covington & Burling (senior Raider Reuben Robertson III was a former member), food marketing for children, and mental health.

The quality of the research in the Nader reports varies. *New Republic's* review of *The Closed Enterprise System* was less than sanguine. Citibank claimed that the students were not sufficiently versed in banking processes to make a substantive critique. *Power And Land In California* drew a host of negative comment from newspapers in that state. Columnist Clark Mollenhoff claimed that the Naider's Raiders report on Delaware, *The Company State,* made a serious error in attacking Senator John Williams for lobbying for legislation which benefited a member of the DuPont family. The reporter said that the legislation had in fact benefited a number of people, of whom one happened to be a DuPont family member.

Another consumer advocate who has worked closely with Nader and the Nader groups in the past offered the following appraisal of the accuracy of reports, with the stipulation that the criticism be unattributed because this person hoped to continue working with Nader and the Nader groups. "We often find that their research has inaccuracies. When he was working on his own he was fine. It's out of his control now, he's got hundreds of people working there with no centralization. The people working for Nader get very little guidance. If they're good, that's great. But there's no attempt to pass on learned methodology. But they're a lot better at getting research and the right people to talk than we are; that alone makes them more valuable."

The consumer advocate told of a lunch he had had with one Nader project director. The director had met twice with Nader. Once the topic was automobiles (not the study group's assignment) and the other was a very general discussion of how the project in question should be undertaken. The study group director knew nothing about the area he was exploring before he went into it. He felt there were errors in the study but "couldn't get enough help from Nader for it. And there didn't seem to be anyone else who knew enough to be helpful."

Generally, the reports have been well-received. The report on the FTC led to a cleaning of house there. So did *The Chemical Feast,* which led to a turnover at the FDA. Other reports have been praised for their thoroughness and attendance to detail. An anti-Nader review in the *New Republic* conceded that the students had done a fine job in *The Closed Enterprise System* of summing up all the existing literature on anti-trust, no mean feat in itself.

The Congress project, however, is the one everyone is looking forward to. It is by far the most exhaustive that Nader has organized to date. To make sure that his other activities are not impeded (there's a possibility of someone trying to take away the Center's tax-exempt status on political grounds because of the unfavorable things the study might turn up), Nader has moved his director of the project, senior Raider Robert Fellmeth and his staff to a suite of a half-dozen freshly painted offices several blocks away.

Fellmeth is a graduate of Stanford and Harvard Law and is a native Hawaiian. At twenty-seven he is one of the youngest of the Nader's senior associates. He takes offense at being called a Raider ("I think it's a bit silly. It sounds like we run all over the place. Going through mounds of reports and compiling very precise research is not exactly a lark.")

Fellmeth, dressed in a corduroy work suit and work-shirt the day we talked to him, is one of the most informal of Nader's associates. He's hard-working (typing furiously when we arrived), fun-loving and with a ready smile. There is nothing in his manner that smacks of nervously trying to "guard Ralph." We talked about his work with Nader, the Nader Mystique, and, of course, the project on Congress.

Q: Tell us about the study of Congress.

A: I can tell you about its scope and how we're recruiting but I can't tell you about its substance—there is no substance yet because the final research hasn't been started yet. There's been preliminary research that's necessary for study. A team of fifteen people have researched the law in specific areas, the law in lobbying, various tax loopholes, systems, and breaks that affect lobbying one way or another. They've researched a number of other questions and written a number of other memos which include: explanation of the law, regulations, leading techniques in the field, major contacts, etc. After that preliminary work had been done we started a library of materials on Congress. Then we started recruiting—we did that over three months. We recruited in the field two groups: one in every state capital for campaign contribution records, which has been going on for about a month, and one person or a team to cover every member of Congress. These people are supplied with packets which instruct them very specifically on what to do, down to opening the telephone book, look under such-and-such and so forth. They do forty to fifty hours worth of research each, some probably doing one hundred hours, concerning each member of each district. They cover the method of campaigning; the amount of information available in that district about Congress; information about that representative; pork barrels; campaign contributions; basis of support; how the district office operates; they interview ten or twelve community leaders, the last major opponent of the member, the leader of the party or faction opposing the member, the leader of the member's own party, local reporters, etc.

All this material will be coming back here to be keypunched and go under files for the individual members of Congress.

The second group of individuals we're recruiting will be journalists. We'll be getting about thirty journalists here in Washington who will go over material coming in from the field, who will verify and re-verify it, filling in the holes. They will then interview the AA and LA of each member of Congress, and interview each member himself. Then, looking at all the material we have gathered, they will put it together in a thirty- to forty-page profile format which will go into a fifteen thousand-page publication.

A third group of eighty to eighty-five individuals will be here in Washington doing research full-time, drawing upon the key-punched information and other sources. Forty-five will be studying committees, forty will be studying such topics as: elections, barriers to new candidates, how competitive are elections, national and given advantages to incumbents, campaign contributions, registration requirements, and the organization of Congress. We'll move into specific suggestions for reform in these areas. The group studying committees will be organized with four to five studying each committee.

There will be eighteen to nineteen teams led by professors or young attorneys working on both topics and committees. The leaders will have some experience in the field but not be identified with a particular party politician, or ideology.

Q: Isn't it going to be difficult to find people like that?

A: No, we have them. It's not too hard—academicians tend to be like that anyway. It was a little hard with the attorneys but we found them, too. Some of them can be identified with conservation issues, but for everyone we had identify with one party we we had another who identified with the other party, so we're in good shape as far as our non-partisanship is concerned.

In terms of the status of the project, most of the people who have been recruited are at work. There are about fifty or sixty missing of the five hundred and thirty-five (NOTE: number of members in

Congress) needed to be covered. All state capitals but one are covered . . . we have accepted about one hundred of one hundred ten people we want down here. They'll work part-time and full-time until the summer, then work full-time in the summer, then back to part-time/full-time.

Q: Is this on a voluntary basis or are some people being paid depending on their job?

A: Need is the criteria in terms of money; if they have money, people are expected to volunteer. If they don't have money they are paid enough to survive, usually for a room and $400 for the summer.

Q: How did you get these people?

A: The people in the field we got by going around to the associates of Nader, and there are about fifty to one hundred of them now in Washington, and asking for suggestions for people for the field—those are volunteers. This is the safest for us, these people we either know or someone we know knows, for they'll be more reliable. The people of D.C. are recruited through placement offices of the universities. We went to the placement offices of thirty to forty universities all over the country and advertised. We went to universities where we have contacts, where people have come from who have already worked for us; we tend to concentrate more on those places where we have someone who can verify a person's capabilities. We interviewed at thirty to thirty-five universities.

Q: Do you have more people volunteering than you need?

A: It depends. Generally we didn't need too many volunteers, especially here in Washington with this staff. Now we need twenty-five to thirty volunteers. We moved and lost people to projects going on at our old place or they moved or something.

Q: Do you have any relationship with the Center for the Study of Responsive Law?

A: No, we have no relationship to the Center. The Center is a tax-exempt educational organization and we are not tax-exempt and are separate in every respect.

Q: How is it that you are not tax-exempt? Are you not a non-profit organization?

A: Most assuredly we are not a profit organization. We're not tax-exempt because we're in a very sensitive area and because, frankly, the Internal Revenue Service could be used as a political device to punish those who are engaged in activities with whom their allies, friends, benefactors, supporters, or those whom they depend upon for support in Congress might find them offensive. That happened with the Sierra Club fighting the Grand Canyon Dam and is too likely for us to take any chances. We're just not taking any chances at all. Furthermore, we want to be free to influence legislation and elections, which we may very well do, and we can't be tax-exempt and do that.

In terms of the money supporting us, it's all coming from Nader's speaking fees so it's all money from Nader personally—no other source.

Q: No other source?

A: No.

Q: Would you want it to come from other sources?

A: I would like the idea of having Public Citizen, Inc. giving us some money. That's non-tax-exempt money we could use and would give me a good feeling to have fifty thousand to one hundred thousand people financing the report. I like the idea. But Ralph feels that he just doesn't want to be put into a situation where anyone has any question at all about where their money is going. For example, what if someone sends in $20 and we say something about his Congressman with which he disagrees—better to have no questions asked. So that money is going into the activities which are enumerated in the Public Citizen brochure. Some people send in money saying, "We heard about your Congress project, feel enthusiastic about it, so here's $20." But he just feels with this study, because it's going to be controversial, that there be no questions. There's going to be many people searching for *ad hominem* attacks so it's best to do nothing about it.

Q: Well, what do you do in a case like the one you exemplified where the money is specified for the Congress project?

A: If the people say this money must be used for the Congress project we'll send it back. If they say "This money is for Public Citizen. Heard about your Congress project—keep it going," which is what usually happens, we'll just use it for other things.

Q: Nader is really closely tied in with this project, right?

A: Oh yes. He's in very close touch from every check that's signed, every person we're recruiting, he knows their resumés, he's talked to most of them (the leaders), in fact, he's tried to recruit most of them himself, he's up to date on the field, he knows exactly what's happening, he discusses policy, he receives Friday memos from everyone working for him on exactly what they're doing. He's very much involved with it.

Q: Do you see him often?

A: Well, we just moved to this location—we don't know if he's going to have an office here or not. He told me he's going to be spending increasing time here as the project develops. He's also talking about renting more room in the same building, in which case he'd probably have an office on another floor so that he could keep in touch with us without being hassled all the time. He's over at the Corporate Accountability Research Group across the street from the Center, and he calls every two or three days for an hour and a half.

Q: How long has he had this project in mind?

A: I'm sure it's been in his mind for a couple of years at least. In terms of actually proposing it, I was leading his California Project at the time in California and had just finished the *Interstate Congress Omission* on the ICC when he mentioned he was interested in doing something on Congress generally. He didn't intimate he wanted me to be the leader at that time; later on he suggested that I lead it and I decided that I couldn't pass up the opportunity—it was going to be too important. I felt a sense of responsibility—because he felt I could do the job, I had to try.

Q: How did you get involved initially with Nader's projects?

A: I was at Harvard Law School and had written to him, along with a friend, and asked him what we could do. This was back in '67. He said come on down and meet with him, so we met in a restaurant some Sunday afternoon. He said "The FTC, I think, has been pulling the wool over a lot of people's eyes. It has a good reputation but I don't think it deserves it and I think it ought to be looked into." What do law students know about the FTC? We didn't, but we went back to Harvard and started doing research on it—the law and the agency. We came back in the summer and started doing our study on it . . . John Schulz, Ed Cox, Will Taft, Andy Egendorf and a few others. Three of us wrote the testimony and delivered it before the Agency and Congress, wrote a report backed up by the ABA, and turned it into a book on the FTC.

The next summer Nader asked me to organize all "Nader's Raiders" so I raised forty thousand dollars or so from foundations, drew up a proposal, got the backing of the Harvard Law Faculty and the Dean, and started recruiting. I recruited about one hundred ten that summer. We came down here and divided into five teams to cover the ICC, FDA, Department of Agriculture, Auto Safety, and air and water pollution. Those teams have produced the books out now.

The following summer he wanted me to go out to California. I took the largest team he's ever assembled, twenty-four, and I think by far his best team which included eight attorneys, a Ph.D. biologist, Austria's leading young city planner, an agricultural economist from Stanford's Food Research Institute, and the number one and number two people from the Harvard Law Review . . . a really top-notch team. The work went easily because the research was of such really high quality. The work was so prodigious, careful, and thorough.

Q: What are the main points of that study?

A: It's a very long report—about three-quarters of a million words. It covers power and land in California, with the fundamental theme that those who control land and depend on land for their personal gain control policy for the state. The loggers control logging laws directly and completely; drillers control mining laws completely; real estate industry controls real estate laws completely; polluters of the state control the pollution laws, which are supposed to be the best in the nation. Right on down the line like that.

Q: Do you feel that's a microcosm of our whole situation?

A: Yes, I think so. I think from the things I've written . . . I've written a section of *With Justice for Some,* which is a book by Mark Green who's over at CARG. They're doing something else. They're writing a charter which is going to require corporations involved in interstate commerce to register or incorporate Federally rather than within one state. Anyway, the book describes just that. [It] describes how private interests have taken over the setting of public policy and the enforcement of law. What has resulted is an industrialist-socialist state, the difference being in socialism the state controls industry and in industrial-socialism, industry controls the state. In the system which I favor, neither controls; the two are separate and distinct and independent from one another. The political system has its own economic base, own sources of information, own basis for making its decisions and yet it relies upon the self-regulating market system to regulate as much as possible. This is the American model but unfortunately is not even close to being in effect anywhere.

Q: Too many people are involved in both aspects and there's a conflict.

A: Yes, there's campaign contributions, lobbying . . . there's IT&T.

Q: Ah, yes, does IT&T serve as more incentive to your project?

A: Well, we've been aware of the existence of IT&T, and lots of things like IT&T exist. In fact, we were involved in the IT&T thing long before Jack Anderson. We knew about much of what Anderson has revealed before he revealed it. Reuben Robertson brought suit against IT&T to block the acquisition of a Hartford insurance firm in court in review of a series of letters and memos which are essentially the same kind of thing.

Q: We were thinking more of trying to reach the people while this is still on their minds.

A: It will help—it focuses attention on corruption. To the extent that we find corruption our allegations will be more believable. Corruption may not be our main theme, however. The kind of corruption I object to anyway is not the Dita Beard kind of corruption. It's institutional corruption. It's not when you have one person taking a bribe; it's when you have nine members of the State Forest Practices of Logging in the state of California consisting of commercial loggers. That's legal corruption! That's it right there.

I'm also more concerned about other questions which seem to me to block public interest legislation and government even without elements of corruption, and you can't pretend even if we had no elements of corruption that everything would be all right. Other things have to be done. There has to be adequate independent information. As long as there's only one or two staff members to cover a wide area, he's not going to get independent information, for he'll have to depend on those that already have the information, and who has that information . . . those organized for personal profit make it their business to have the information.

So you have the question of information flow, of proper sanctions, of the competitiveness of elections, questions of visibility and accountability . . . all sorts of questions which relate to institutional corruption and are equally important.

We're going to try to get all the barriers if we can and set forth proposals that will wipe them all out in one blow.

Q: There's something that I've noticed in talking to people involved in Nader's operation—the tone of optimism. Do you really think you're going to change things?

A: Naivete is a pedagogical device—like in *Candide,* a kind of innocence that leads you to believe. You are told that everyone wants billboards taken down for more beautiful roads, then are surprised when you discover that on public, Federally-owned land the government is charging one-tenth the amount of money to people who are building and leasing billboards as private owners are. They are actually subsidizing it. You're shocked. If you don't have any shock you don't have any effect in terms of your writing, no sense of persuasion.

These things are too important to give up on. We're not talking about sports. We're talking about whether people are going to live or die, get decent educations, are going to be healthy . . . these are basics. You just can't say forget it.

Most of us are very honest in our view that we're longshots. We're in a very delicate spot and depend on things for support which we can't always count on. We depend on the media for support, but there are problems with some media.

We're reaching a point right now where it's becoming fashionable to attack Ralph Nader, and I think that's going to increase. Some of it is press jealousy. But it's always news in the media when the boy bites the dog, so to speak; another report coming out with Ralph Nader criticizing something is expected. So what becomes news is something being wrong with the report or its methods or him.

This results in absurd kinds of media results. For example, in California we devastatingly documented a single 102 million-dollar California land fraud . . . hardly a mention of it anywhere. Instead there was a long front-page article on the fact that we did not interview then Deputy Attorney General O'Brien, a California figure, before we published a few sentences about him, which in fact we had. The point is that the focus and intent was on us—personalities, not fact.

It's as if there's no outside world—that everything is okay in America—that they're not doing anything to the land in California, the streams are perfectly clean and not being polluted, that people are not being poisoned with pesticides. These things are getting less and less attention while the question of self-aggrandizing is getting more. I think the analogy might be if media went in to interview James Roche and his relationship with his second vice-president, rather than how the products of GM affect people. There's a cult in this country that is very interested in personality . . . whether someone is nice to someone else, has lovers or not, etc. We see increasing attention being given to us in these catagories and less and less to the issues that affect people's lives, and this is frustrating. That's a phenomenon that happens when you have a personality like Ralph Nader.

Q: Could your office continue if Ralph Nader should suddenly leave? Would it be as effective without him or do you think his charisma is part of the incredible impact?

A: His charisma comes in handy for press releases. In terms of charisma he's the best press agent in Washington. His contribution is important. I'm sure most of us would be doing the same thing at this point even if he didn't exist, anyhow. I mean, we'll stay in touch with him but if he weren't in existence we wouldn't change our plans at all.

Q: What about the California case where the facts were devastating, as you said, and still received poor coverage. If you didn't have someone like Ralph Nader to spearhead the group, who would ever hear about these things?

A: Right. Nader got good national press to counteract bad local press in California. We wouldn't have had that without him. I think he's trying to begin to give us an identity. "Nader's Raiders" would go on; it already has an identity. You'd probably find fifteen to twenty-five percent less coverage; people would have to work harder. But the value would be not to have one person to focus on. People don't focus on Jim Roche or Henry Ford and say "what's he doing at night?" There's a big advantage to that in terms of defense. In a sense we're very vulnerable. We're vulnerable to *ad hominem* attack, personification. . .

Q: Do you think the movement is in danger of becoming too bureaucratized?

A: There was a stage about a year ago where it was beginning to move too fast. Now we're retrenching a little bit—this is the only major study that's going to be going on. Now Nader is relying on decentralization, on starting self-generating groups. Once he sets up other people in other places on their own with their own identity and power in every state capitol, he'll be all set. That will give the movement its strength. Each student will be giving three dollars a semester to start their own action arm in every state capitol. In California there are two lobbyists representing every kind of conservation imaginable; there are two hundred thirty-five on the other side. With the California Action Arm there could be fifty to sixty on the other side of the ledger. That kind of balance of power change could make an enormous difference, especially with those fifty or sixty putting out twice as much effort as those on the other side.

The key is retrenching, focusing on two or three major projects, and following up effectively and continuously, such as the tax PIRG (Public Interest Research Group). The summer activities should level off at one hundred people, for much more is too many for Ralph or anyone to really handle as well as he should.

Q: Couldn't there be other people equally in charge of the programs?

A: Ralph relies a great deal on his directors; he always has. Nevertheless, it is his name and in order to know what everyone is doing, he's got to keep it to a manageable size.

Q: Some people are just waiting for him to slip up.

A: Oh sure. One person stealing a document, hitting an official, offering a bribe, etc., even a report with errors could hurt very, very seriously. In fact, they're trying to do it—they're making up errors, distorting reports to a great extent, lying about them, imputing our motives. This is a good sign, however; it means we're being believed and are effective.

Q: In a different vein, I suppose you must like Ralph Nader or you wouldn't be working for him. . .

A: Well, actually I probably would even if I didn't like him, which I do, because I like what he's doing. I believe in his values and cause. He has a very sophisticated philosophy which is not articulated, because there's no reason to make enemies or friends based on pure abstractions which have no meaning. So instead of abstracting his political philosophy it must be imputed from separate statements, but I know what it is and I agree with it. I have the same utopian model as he does, and that's what attracts me to him. As far as his personal magnetism, he's an extraordinary man. He reads five thousand words a minute, speaks several languages including either Chinese or Arabic, one of those very difficult ones. He has almost a photographic memory. He's a very good and eloquent writer with a unique style. He's a brilliant speaker, a shy man, and has an extraordinarily good sense of humor, although he is not portrayed that way. In the press he appears very close-mouthed and stern but in fact is really a very happy kind of laughing person. Most of his humor is involved with the issues—the things people do, things people try to pull. He's not at all a down-mouthed serious individual—on the contrary, he laughs more than most people I know.

Q: Do you think that because so much of his life centers around these topics that his humor will naturally do this also?

A: Oh yes. Sometimes it doesn't, but mostly it is about what he's talking about at the time or personalities involved. For instance, I talk very fast, so he talks as fast as he possibly can just to tease me, sometimes so quickly that I can hardly understand him. Whenever we have a conversation he ends it with a long monologue and hangs up on me real quick. When I talk with him I fire things to him, not wanting to take up his time; things get direct and businesslike, so he teases me about it.

Q: What about his image as an ascetic—is that correct?

A: Oh, that's true. It's funny though; why don't people wonder about priests?

Lowell Dodge, thirty-two, who heads Nader's Center for Auto Safety is a graduate of Yale and Harvard Law School and a former civil rights worker in the South. The Center for Auto Safety was established in April of 1968 with a financial boost from Consumer's Union. The main task facing its six man staff (including two attorneys and an engineer) is the monitoring of the National Highway Traffic Safety Administration (NHTSA) which was created by Congress in 1966 to help end auto carnage. By any count, this regulatory agency has been a failure. Any credit for its limited effectiveness must go to the Nader-organized consumer group which has prodded it into action on a number of occasions. There was a slight drop in the number of auto deaths from 56,000 in 1969 to 54,800 in 1970.

The Center is orientated toward eliminating vehicle design defects rather than the behavior behind the wheel of the individual driver. If the machine you're driving is defective it doesn't matter how good a driver you may be.

The non-profit, tax-exempt center sees four main functions for itself. First, as an auto safety advocate. Here the center monitors the regulatory agencies charged with protecting the driver from his vehicle. While the automakers press the various regulatory agencies in their behalf, the Center does likewise or the consumer. According to the Center, "our participation takes the form of docket submissions, petitions for rulemaking, presentations at public meetings and publications. Occasionally, when stronger action is required, the Center institutes legal action."

Secondly, the Center acts as a consumer advocate receiving complaints from car owners about their vehicles. When a defect appears a significant number of times, Dodge and his staff take their data to the National Highway Traffic Administration which has the power to compel manufacturers to issue recall notices. In addition, *What To Do With Your Bad Car* was written by Dodge with Nader and engineer Ralf Hotchkiss, (who is Director of the Nader-backed Center for Concerned Engineering, a direct adjunct to the auto center) is a guerrilla manual for car owners who can't get direct satisfaction from their dealer. The Center has 21,000 consumer complaints about their cars on file. About 250 new oncs are received each week.

A letter from a bakery truck driver tipped the center about defective truck wheels. It took a year, but the center was finally able to get the NHTSA to get GM to issue recalls for the 200,000 bad wheels. Twelve thousand Buicks went back for a look after a letter complaining of a sticking accelerator was received by the Center.

The Center is also becoming a repository for materials concerning auto safety. In its files is information on accidents, injuries, civil suits, government action, recalls, etc. Finally the Center assesses developments in auto safety issuing fact sheets on the newest type of air bags, for example.

The Center's expenses run roughly $35,000 a year. The NHTSA, by contrast, has over six hundred employees and a ninety-million-dollar annual budget. Dodge's salary is in the five figure bracket. Other full-time salaries for the center average about $50 weekly.

Besides the Center for Concerned Engineering, there is Professionals for Auto Safety run by Collot Bruce, a twenty-four-year-old Washington law student. The group is a list of those who stand ready to provide and advise Nader on various aspects of auto safety.

The Corporate Accountability Research Group, or CARG as it is known inside the Nader nation, was established to concentrate on anti-trust matters. The group says it is "concerned with the study of corporate power, the economic concentration and ramifications of market dominance and the means of restraining such power (present and potential). To effect corporate accountability and responsibility, the group is seeking to introduce anti-trust statutes and regulations and insure the enforcement of existing ones."

The group is also handling another one of Nader's pet projects: Federal chartering of the country's one thousand largest companies.

Analytical reports will be issued by the group. Under its sponsorship *The Closed Enterprise System* was completed. It was scheduled to be released in 1972 by Grossman Publishers. A second volume dealing with the regulatory agencies and their role in anti-trust will be published later.

The group has litigated on corporate matters of consumer interest in the past and hopes to improve its impact here. Since CARG does not have tax-exempt status it will be free to lobby and influence the course of antitrust legislation.

Among the staff members are the project director for *The Closed Enterprise System,* Mark Green, a twenty-six-year-old attorney; the associate director of that project, attorney Beverly C. Moore Jr.; Irene Till, an economist; Peter J. Petkas, an attorney; Donald Etra, an attorney; and Craig Kubey, a research assistant.

The Project on Corporate Responsibility is an outgrowth of Campaign GMs of 1970 and 1971, which, though they were endorsed by Nader, were not started by him. Campaign GM wanted the appointment of three independent directors to the GM board, disclosure of detailed information of emission control, auto safety, minority employment and recall campaigns. GM was successful in beating back the upstarts but the company's executive hierarchy took to the hustings to cover their flank. According to Anthony DeLorenzo, public relations vice president for GM, the company's chairman, vice chairman and president made a total of eighty-one speeches and held thirty-six interviews in an attempt to get their side of the story told. Campaign GM may have failed in its specific goals but it flushed the enemy from the woodwork.

A top Nader Associate, John Esposito, who is a senior Raider at the Center for the Study of Responsive Law and who wrote *Vanishing Air,* is a member of the board of the Project on Corporate Responsibility. The concerns of the Project are linked philosophically to everything that Nader has espoused since he first mounted his auto safty campaign and started investigating the nature of corporate policy.

The Aviation Consumer Action Project, yet another Nader spinoff, got its start with $10,000 in Nader seed money in mid-1970. The project was formed "to provide an effective voice for environmental and consumer concerns in aviation. It [was] formed at the urging of concerned citizens around the world—businessmen, doctors, housewives, lawyers, environmentalists, aircraft owners, economists and students . . . as well as pilots, stewardesses and other airline employees." Though Nader is the nominal head of the group, his chief overseer is Reuben Robertson III. Robertson is chairman of the CAB's consumer advisory committee.

The functional head of ACAP is K.G.J. Pillai, also a member of the CAB's advisory board. Pillai wrote a book called *Airnet* which purported to describe cartel arrangements among international airlines. Other directors included Gladys Kessler, an environmental protection lawyer and Wiliam Michael Reisman, a Yale Law School professor who is an expert in international law.

The group hopes to support itself through public contributions, and subscriptions are arranged on a sliding scale from "charter supporter" at $500 to supporter at $10.

Some of the initial forays against the CAB and FAA that the group has mapped out include an investigation into higher air fares, lost baggage (it happens to 200,000 people a year, according to ACAP), overbooked flights, the elimination of price competition, limited airline liability in crashes, a variety of airplane safety violations, and health and environmental pollution safeguards.

One ACAP horror story has to do with the pilot for a major airline who refused to fly a passenger plane because he considered weather conditions unsafe. Incredibly, the company grounded him for fifteen days without pay for "disregard for the economic impact upon the company." The FAA did not challenge the suspension.

You're a fisherman, but all your old haunts are polluted now. You've enjoyed the serenity of spending many a morning angling and then coming home and eating your catch. But there's no catch anymore and the number of pleasant mornings is dwindling. In an effort to stir the public over the clean water issue Nader hit upon a novel idea—go to those who have a great deal to lose if something isn't done—both sport and commercial fishermen.

On July 24, 1971 Nader announced the Fisherman's Clean Water Action Project. He named David Zwick, thirty, who had headed the task force which produced *Water Wasteland,* as coordinator for the group. Montreal Canadians goalie Ken Dryden spent his summer helping on the project.

Nader hoped to get the sixty million fishermen in the country into a broad coalition composed of five or six regional groups, with a central nerve center in Washington. He said that he and the Washington group would help the regional groups get the professionals they needed to assist them in their area—lawyers, engineers, scientists and economists. They would provide the groups with information on water pollution control.

Nader told the *New York Times* that the project would need about 2.5 million dollars to set up the regional centers and the national headquarters.

A Nader's Raider conjures up the image of a young college or professional student but Ralph Nader has taken steps toward breaking that stereotype. In February of 1972 he announced the formation of a Retired Professionals' Action Group.

Some twenty million Americans are sixty-five or over and another twenty-five million are over fifty. Some $40,000 was raised through public subscription to fund the group. Charles E. Adkins, sixty-two, former president of Briarcliff College, was appointed by Nader to head the group. Assisting him as staff associate will be Elma Griesel, thirty, who has worked on the problems of the aged in the past.

Nader said that a permanent staff of ten would be assembled but that he expected a great many volunteers. Three other staff members are Edmond Kanwit, a social economist, Edwin Patterson, a legal consultant on veteran's affairs and Edgar McKean, an accountant.

Older people are a valuable resource according to Nader:

"With shorter retirements and more people being able to retire from their professions, the problem of living useful lives in still alert years is also a problem of underutilizing potentially valuable human resources for a better society. Leisure time, experience, community contacts, often sufficient financial security, family grown up, and a situational potential for free thinking unencumbered by anticipatory ambitions or institutional restrictions all combine to support the likelihood and impact of such groups. Ideally, they can be established all over the country, particularly in heavy retirement areas and Washington, D.C. They can include all skills such as accountants, financial analysts, physicians, lawyers, engineers, scientists, statisticians, writers, etc. At first it would be advisable for them to concentrate on special problems of the elderly—social security, consumer fraud, housing, taxes, medical care, nursing homes, pensions—but soon it would become apparent that our problems are seamless and ageless . . ."

Nader also hoped that the D.C. group would be a prototype and generate similar groups around the country, which would act independently on problems indigenous to the aged and their respective communities. The Washington group, however, would function as liaison with all the other grass roots groups.

Some of the activities that Nader envisioned the Retired Professionals working on included: nursing homes (his own younger Raiders completed the favorably received *Old Age: The Last Segregation* which had some rather horrifying stories about conditions in nursing homes) employment, transportation, and retirement income.

In addition to research activities the Washington group would monitor government regulatory agencies which administer those services which directly affect the aged. They would also develop and prepare critiques on legislation affecting the aged. Two representatives from the group attended the White House Conference on Aging for a start.

Nader said he hoped the group would serve as a valuable alternative to all those old people "who are tired of playing shuffleboard."

Besides the Center for the Study of Responsive Law, Nader's other largest ongoing project is his Public Interest Research Group (PIRG), set up in mid-1970. At any one time it consists of twelve to twenty young lawyers and professionals, usually, in their twenties, who sign on for a year or more at a salary of $4,500.

PIRG does not have tax-exempt status and therefore is free to lobby and litigate as it pleases. If the object of the Center's activities can be said to be producing research, PIRG's aim may be catalogued as getting results.

PIRG lawyers have petitioned the FDA for better labelling of birth control pills, and petitioned the FTC to get detergent makers to list the phosphate content of their product on their packages. They have hassled the government over credit reporting practices and over the way mortgage forms are handled.

If another Nader group needs a suit started, PIRG often handles it but if a protracted court battle seems in the offing, PIRG will look around for a special interest group to carry forth the fight. PIRG will not litigate just for the sake of litigating; it finds that extremely wasteful of both its manpower resources and its budget. PIRG costs roughly $200,000 annually to fund. Nader underwrote the first year from his GM settlement but hopes to finance future years through public contributions.

Sam Simon, a graduate of the University of Texas Law School, headed up PIRG's property tax project and was the editor of the project's newsletter. Simon was the prototype of a PIRG lawyer. At the age of twenty-five he joined Nader for a year at a salary of $4,500. He is married and has a small son.

"In law school," he told reporter Nan Robertson, "I didn't know what I wanted to do—I didn't want to sell out to a big law firm and get lost in the corporate maze or government."

He became aware of PIRG through posters on the Texas campus. After a telephone interview with Nader, he was hired. The property tax project and newsletter that he headed flourished. Washington PIRG put many local tax groups in touch with each other and made it easier for them to swap information.

PIRG, as well as serving as a clearinghouse, supplied the grass roots groups with novel approaches to assessments and tax reform. It provided the groups with a comprehensive bibliography in the area and advised them to read carefully all the local statutes regarding property, as well as checking out specific assessments of individual homeowners and businesses in their communities. The newsletter began in the fall of 1970 and appeared monthly thereafter. Simon, unfortunately, had to leave PIRG to complete his military commitment. But largely due to the project's aggressive efforts, Nader wrought a promise from Senator Edmund Muskie to hold hearings on the property tax.

Two other PIRG lawyers, William Osborne and Larry Silverman relocated in Anmoore, West Virginia (population: 1,000) and went to work on Union Carbide. Their object: to mobilize the community against Union Carbide's pollution of the air. The company's plant there emitted an ash product which blackens buildings, rots cars, and kills other forms of animal and plant life. Nader gave Silverman, who had worked with John Esposito on

Vanishing Air, and Osborne, an ex-VISTA worker, some $5,000 to mount their entire campaign. As a result of the duo's dogged efforts the company said it would clean up its polluting plants and pay higher taxes.

James Welch, a lawyer from the University of Texas, and Donald Ross, a young attorney from New York University, convinced Nader of the efficacy of setting up student PIRG groups around the country, similar to the original Nader had started in Washington. The pair hopscotched the country in 1971 bringing the PIRG gospel to campus after campus. The basic plan is simple: students are assessed $3 or $4 yearly which comes out of the fees they pay their school.

This only happens, however, after a majority of students petition the student senate, board of regents, or other decision-making body with the power to levy such a fee. The money is then used to hire a staff of lawyers, scientists and engineers to work full-time for the local PIRGs. An elected board of students monitor the professionals. Since the professionals are full-time and past college age they forego interruptions like classes, exams, and vacation breaks. They provide a continuity to the projects that the students would be unable to provide and they are best able to make use of student resources on campus. "This approach," reasons PIRG's founders, "enables students to contribute to social problems in a manner which benefits rather than interrupts their education."

Nader, Ross and Welch feel that as unions and corporations have their lobbyists, students should also finance their own "lobbyists" to present their side of the story to government.

The Nader plan provides for rebate to those students who do not wish to participate. The refund provision was included to provide against coercion of the minority. But for the plan to work initially, fifty percent of those voting would have to approve it.

Response to student PIRGs has thus far been good. In Oregon about 30,000 students petitioned the State Board of Higher Education to approve their plan. As a result, about $200,000 was collected at fourteen state colleges and universities to finance the Oregon Student

Public Interest Research Group. Students pay $1 a quarter or $1.50 a semester.

Over 50,000 Minnesota students signed petitions calling for the creation of the Minnesota Public Interest Research Group (MPIRG). Legislative support was lent to the idea in Minnesota and it passed. Students pay $3 a semester.

Nader says that the eight million students at 2,000 colleges and universities could finance 160 PIRGS with $200,000 annual budgets. Comments PIRG: "If even a third of all students participated, a whole new dimension would be added to the political life of the United States . . . No longer would decisions affecting students be made in isolation."

Presently PIRGs are aborning or being formed in the following areas: Rhode Island, Western Massachusetts, Eastern Massachusetts, Vermont, Ohio, Western Pennsylvania, New Jersey, South Carolina, the District of Columbia, Delaware, Texas, San Diego, California, West Virginia, Washington, Hawaii, Utah, Illinois, Missouri and Georgia.

Some of the issues that Nader hopes the local groups will attack are property tax, occupational safety and health, employment discrimination, the environment, retail pricing, and other issues of a general consumer nature.

Nader and Ross wrote a manual for organizing PIRGs called *Action For A Change* which Grossman published in 1971. The book dealt with mechanics of organizing interest in PIRGs, funding them, getting a staff and projects to tackle.

One of the most interesting PIRGS is a non-student affiliated group in Connecticut called the Connecticut Citizens Action Group (formerly the Connecticut Earth Action Project).

Ross and Welch worked with local people and raised over $50,000 to fund the group. The average contribution was 70¢. It was raised through bake sales, car washes, even door to door. The group is headed by twenty-seven-year-old Toby Moffet, a native of Connecticut and former Director of the Office of Students and Youth in the Department of Health, Education and Welfare. He became director in September 1969 and quit after the Cambodian incursion in 1970. Though not a lawyer, Moffet has had a wealth of administrative experience even at this young age. He is one of the few top Nader operatives who is not a lawyer.

The offices of the CCAG in downtown Hartford sit directly across from the Hartford Fire Insurance Company, whose merger with IT&T Nader tried to block. It's as though Ralph Nader has his own personal vantage point to keep an eye on Hartford Fire. Besides having its main office in Hartford the group also has regional offices in New Haven and Greenwich.

Moffet met Nader when both were speaking on programs at Syracuse University. They had dinner and Moffet, suitably impressed, kept in touch with Nader while he was at HEW.

CCAG has ten full-time staff members including two attorneys and several former VISTA volunteers. The average age is middle to late twenties. Salaries for professionals average $4,000 full-time yearly. "And I mean full-time," says Moffet, "Look, there's no use in paying more, I always say, there's no time to spend it anyway."

CCAG made great waves when it found Colt workers who told of operational deficiencies in the Colt M-16 rifle. This sparked Congressional ire and became a national story rather than just one of local significance.

The find came about when University of Connecticut law student William Sklar, twenty-three, was looking into how the state's occupational health and safety law was being administered. There were rumors of lead poisoning (Colt workers fire the guns to make sure if they work and dust is given off.) Sklar found a man willing to talk about the lead poisoning. He went to the man's house and interviewed him and as he was leaving the man said, "Hey, if you really want a story," and then told him how workers were being ordered to cheat on accuracy tests by the company.

"I was a bit skeptical at first," admits Moffit. "We don't like to take a chance on having wrong information, so I asked Bill if we could get more information. In the course of two weeks we got five more affidavits from workers."

The report called *The M-16: Colt's Lethal Lemon* was released November 1, 1971.

The inspection process calls for sample rifles to be taken from each shipment of 6,000. If the sample rifles fail, the whole shipment must be reprocessed. One worker claimed: "After every thousand rounds or so we tell Mr. Ivy (the range supervisor) what sort of problems we have covered up in the last series. Parts, including carriers, extractor springs, and bolts, are switched on the endurance gun, out of sight of Government men." Colt had produced to that point some 2.5 million M-16's at a cost of about 250 million dollars.

Besides the part changing, the report said that barrels were bent. The report also claimed that government inspectors could not have been aware of Colt's actions.

Said the report: "If Colt exhibited the dedication and throughness in producing a reliable rifle that it exhibited in subverting the testing process, there can be little doubt that few weapon failures would occur in combat."

CCAG recommended the following remedial actions:

1. A Department of Justice investigation of the comany's activities.

2. House and Senate hearings to examine "these derelictions which affect the safety of our troops."

3. Examination of the Federal inspection system which is supposed to exercise quality control over the rifles.

4. A determination as to whether Colt should be able to bid or receive other government contracts.

5. Examination of all of Colt's testing procedures and production methods.

6. That the company be prohibited from taking sanctions against the "whistleblowing" employees.

The report summarized its findings this way:

"In a situation where both honest and competent management were required, deception, fraud, and negligence occurred. Greed, incompetence, apathy and dishonesty are factors. However, the soldiers in Vietnam were also victims of concentrated yet unaccountable corporate power, a type of institutional and personal lawlessness which is not often enough seen for the crime that it is."

Colt denied the charges but Connecticut Senator Abraham Ribicoff and Representative William Cotter both called for the Senate Armed Services Committee to look into the matter immediately.

CCAG has also instituted a vigorous anti-highway lobby called the Committee to Change Transportation Priorities, headed by twenty-four-year-old Dennis Chapman, a former Pennsylvania VISTA worker. The group, led by Chapman, watches out for consumer interests in the highway areas. For one hearing 600 people were bused into the state capitol, stunning both legislators and press.

Other CCAG projects include the problem of power plant sites, air pollution, telephone rate hikes, property tax, TV ecology ads, and solid waste disposal problems.

Another CCAG prototype is the Connecticut Citizens lobby headed by twenty-five-year-old Angie Martin, another former VISTA volunteer. She divided the state into twenty-two regions by phone exchange, so that none of her regional mobilizers would have to make a collect call. Each district has a coordinator, and twenty-five other people who each have five people to call. So in each district of the state there are 125 in a region, so that there are 2,500 people state-wide to date. Says Moffet, "We mobilize those people at the drop of a hat. They write letters. They write the Governor, their legislator. When these people write letters they know that hundreds of others are also writing letters. They've really been phenomenal. We have had good success with them on four or five issues, like the air implementation plan that that state has to establish under the Federal clean air law of 1970. We packed three public hearings on the plan here. We produced expert witnesses. It's quite obvious that citizen pressure had a calculable effect on these things."

The apotheosis of all the Nader groups is Public Citizen, Inc., a national citizens organization which Nader has attempted to fuel through full page advertisements in *The New York Times* and a heavy direct mail campaign. For $15, you can become a "public citizen."

Part of Nader's mail appeal went as follows:

"Let's suppose that a strong, citizen movement had begun in America, say, twenty-five years ago; a public interest movement which required industry and government to be responsive to the just needs and aspirations of all the people.

Think what might have been accomplished during these years of unprecedented national economic growth if public-spirited values were applied to such aggregate affluence:

—We would have discovered the hunger and poverty of the "other America" long before the Sixties and reduced this massive suffering in a land of plenty.

—Our urban centers would not be choking with cars on concrete belts carving up polluted cities filled with slums, corruption, crime and public waste.

—Consumers would not be cheated by "planned obsolescence," price-fixing, and goods and services which, according to Senator Philip Hart's studies, take at least twenty-five percent of every consumer dollar without returning any value.

—There would be far fewer inequities in our income and property tax laws. Why should a factory or office worker pay twenty percent of his wages while men of great wealth are often assessed four percent—or less—of their income? Why should small businessmen and homeowners pay far more than their fair share of taxes because large corporate property owners of land, minerals and buildings pay far less than prevailing assessments require?

—Our rivers, lakes and oceans would still be safe for swimming and would be producing untainted fish; the air would not be as filled with violent contamination and the land not abused with the ravages and spills of insensitive corporate and governmental forces.

—Thousands of Americans would not be dying or made sick each year from unsafe working conditions that too often prevail in factories, foundries and mines filled with toxic chemicals, gases and dust.

—Equal opportunity in education and employment and

adequate medical care would have avoided the misery that cruelly affects many Americans.
that cruelly affects many Americans.
and their civilian superiors might have been closely examined and modified long ago.

And if the prospective citizen is suitably impressed he mails off his contribution and that's the last he hears, because the mailing piece has already told him: "Please don't send me a thank-you note or additional literature. I know what's wrong. What I want to see is something done about it."

The hard sell worked pretty well. In the first seven months Nader received some $642,040 from 42,000 contributors for Public Citizen, Inc. Advertising and printing expenses ran $180,810, leaving a net profit of $461,230.

Nader said in March 1972 that he was going to use the funds to underwrite the Retired Professionals Action Group, the Tax Reform Research Group, and a new health research group composed of doctors, lawyers and scientists. Public Citizen also gave a $10,00 grant to the Center for Women Policy Studies, which operates independently of Nader.

Public Citizen has undertaken two major Nader suits to date. The first was against price fixing and anti-trust against the milk producers and The White House. The second charged the Justice Department with failure to enforce Federal election laws.

Nader For The Consumer

The consumer is at the mercy of business in the marketplace. He can choose or not choose to purchase a particular product—that is his only option. If he opts to purchase goods which he knows are adulterated or inferior it is usually out of necessity.

Nader's trenchant attacks on the two agencies most responsible for safeguarding the consumer's wellbeing—the Federal Trade Commission and the Food and Drug Administration—have produced a very tangible benefit for the consumer. If a product has been misrepresented, or found to be deficient in some aspect, Nader's goading of the agency under whose jurisdiction the problem falls has often remedied the situation.

But Nader has made clear the fact that both agencies can do more. Congressmen like Benjamin Rosenthal have echoed Nader's sentiments. He has charged the FDA with not letting consumers know the names of products which may be health hazards. He has called on the FDA to release "complete and up-to-date lists" of all consumer products containing possibly harmful ingredients.

The first group of Nader's Raiders including Edward Cox, son-in-law of Richard M. Nixon, investigated the Federal Trade Commission in the summer of 1968. (The two Raiders who co-authored the FTC critique with Cox were Robert C. Fellmeth and John Schulz.) These three original Raiders found the FTC to be an inperturbable crony-infested bureaucracy doing virtually nothing for the consumer. As a result, Nixon turned out many of the long-time fixtures (relics of the New Deal) and replaced them with younger and more vigorous men, who in turn were not immune to Nader's ire.

The FTC came into being with the Clayton Anti-Trust Act of 1914. Its primary responsibility was to see that no monopolies materialized in front of its eyes. In 1938, the Wheeler-Lea Act gave the FTC the power to look into deceptive practices. The FTC got added power and burdens through the passage of the 1953 Flammable Fabrics Act and the Fair Packaging and Labeling Act of 1966.

The forerunner of the FDA was presaged in the Pure Food and Drug Act of 1906. The Act prohibited using dangerous additives in food and drugs as well as adulterants used to conceal inferior product quality. This Act was expended and revised when the Pure Food Drug and Cosmetic Act was passed in 1938. New regulations on theraputic devices and cosmetics were covered. The act also made it mandatory for the FDA to approve any new drug before it was put on the market.

A 1969 summer study of the FDA by Raider James Turner and associates produced *The Chemical Feast*. Not surprising was the report's conclusion that the FDA had been lax in exercising its prerogatives to protect the consumer. The report picked out several monumental areas of intransigence including the banning of cyclamates and the unregulated use of MSG as a food additive. By January of 1970 Richard Nixon had replaced three top men at FDA.

Before launching into a full-scale discussion of the inter-relationship of the consumer and his erstwhile protectors, it's helpful to enumerate two of the most common and most misused aspects of the FDA's consumer protection powers.

First is an amendment to the Pure Food and Drug Act known as the Delaney Clause, named after the New York State congressman who sponsored it. The amendment, passed in 1958, provides that any additive which has proven to have caused cancer in men or animals is deemed unsafe and cannot be added to a particular product. It was under the provisions of this clause that the HEW Secretary finally withdrew cyclamates from general consumer consumption in 1969, even though equivocal results showed that tumors in laboratory animals had been caused by the substances as early as 1950. Roughly speaking, the clause works when it works. It has been applied with a distressing lack of uniformity since its enactment in 1958.

The other booby trap which is supposed to safeguard consumer interests is the Generally Recognized As Safe (GRAS) list. The 1958 Food Additives Amendment called for additives to be proven safe before being sanctioned for general use in our food supply. Rigorous testing was to be the criteria by which the substances were to be found safe or unsafe.

Instead the FDA drew up a list of almost 200 common additives and circulated them to 900 scientists asking them if the substances on the list were generally recognized as being safe for human consumption. Only thirty-nine percent of those consulted bothered to answer the FDA inquiry. Slightly over half who responded called all the substances safe or made no comment. Some 156 scientists questioned one or more substances on the list. A half-dozen substances were deleted from the list, and the resulting items comprised the GRAS list. Cyclamates were a group of additives that were questioned by a number of the scientists, but they were left on. So, research scientists or consumers who questioned the FDA about the safety of cyclamates were told that the substance was "generally recognized as safe."

Now the law provided scientific testing to determine if the substances were, indeed, safe. It made no mention of a one-time mailing to a group of experts—fine men though they may be.

Food additives are by no means a new phenomenon. From antiquity different types of foodstuffs have been preserved with incidental additives that resulted from cooking. Pickling, fermenting, salting, and smoking date back hundreds of years. The Chinese used kerosene to ripen bananas. The Egyptians invented food colors. But many common substances were adulterated then as now, including tea, coffee, wine, bread, beer and spices. Generally additives fall into four broad classes: flavoring agents, coloring agents, texture agents, and preservatives. All four groups contain elements that can be used in combination so as to present a health hazard.

Fortune magazine estimates that consumers ingest more than one billion pounds of additives annually at a cost of 500 million dollars. These 1,800 substances, according to *Fortune,* work out to something like five pounds a head of additives per year. A number of additives have been linked to carcinogens, teratogens and mutagens. For instance, sodium nitrate used to cure pork products can form a dangerous amine compound which is a known carcinogen (a cancer-producing substance). Certain food colors are suspected teratogens (substances which impair the genetic function of cells). However, no food additive to date has been certified as a mutagen (a substance producing a permanent genetic condition in which deformed traits or abnormalities are handed from generation to generation).

The problem of additives is disturbing even in the abstract. In the midst of the organic renaissance we are undergoing in our consumption of foodstuffs, it has become doubly so. If a particular food product is not ready for consumption in its natural state, what justification is there for adulterating it—even with the benefits of modern technology? The proliferation of organic food stores and co-ops throughout the country is a significant nay-saying to the food industry, and its attempts to color, flavor and market processed taste.

The Delany Clause and the GRAS, both instituted

with the consumer's safety in mind, have been signal and dismal failures.

Below are enumerated in detail some of the more intransigent instances when additives and adulterants posed serious questions about consumer safety, corporate arrogance and bureaucratic indolence. Nader's Raiders led by James Turner, who wrote *The Chemical Feast,* a critical history of the FDA, have documented hundreds of instances where the FDA failed to act in accordance with the powers granted it under law and therefore exposed the public unnecessarily to grave danger.

On February 13, 1972, Senator Gaylord Nelson of Wisconsin, who in the past had been closely allied with various Nader causes, asked that the FDA be given broader powers in regard to regulating additives that find their way into our foodstuffs. The Senator's sentiments are well taken, but in view of the regulatory role by the FDA in the past it hardly seems necessary to give the FDA more power to do less with.

Nelson said he was ready to introduce a bill which would make it mandatory that additives be proven safe before they could be generally used in foods. "We are being chemically medicated against our will," said Nelson as he took dead aim at preservatives, stabilizers, extenders, antitoxidants, emulsifiers, bleaches, conditioners, sweeteners, coloring agents, flavoring agents, and other possible additives. Borrowing on another well-used analogy, Nelson spoke of a food-industrial complex which needed close regulation for the consumer by the FDA. Without pinpointing any single additive, Nelson said: "[there are] a proliferation of food chemicals that are unnecessary, many of them untested, some of them dangerous and most of them poorly monitored, at best."

Some 1,600,000 pounds of additives are added to our food yearly. There are some 3,000 different ones—1,000 in direct use and the rest in packing, fertilizers, pesticides, etc. Only about 700 of this number are on the GRAS list, the flimsy consumer backstop currently used as a standard.

The Nelson legislation called for all testing to be done immediately and the tab to be picked up by the maker.

All results would become a matter of public record. The criteria for approval would be a substantial nutritive or qualitative improvement and/or lowering in price of the foodstuffs in question.

In partial response to Nader's prodding, the FDA has at least known where to look for figurative needles in haystacks. The GRAS list and the Delaney Clause have too many loopholes to be considered effective and the FDA, for all its recent vigilance on the additive problem, still moves too much to the beat of business's tune.

On January 31, 1972, the FDA moved against antibiotics in livestock feed—but only in the most timid fashion. FDA Commissioner Charles C. Edwards, not a charter member of the Ralph Nader Fan Club, said the feeds were not an iminent hazard but were in his words, "a very real potential health hazard." The drug-hyped feeds result in an annual bonanza of some 400 million dollars to livestock producers because the feeds tend to nurture bigger animals. The FDA copped out by throwing in sixty days for public comment—long enough to catalogue all the industry response—and promised that in no event would controls be instituted before January 1, 1973.

Better than three-fourths of all meat that ends up on our dinner tables is medicated prior to its arrival there, according to the FDA. Like the cyclamate problem, the feed problem did not materialize overnight. The antibiotics have been a part of feeds since after World War II.

More than 1,000 drug compounds faced FDA action because of lack of adequate research data. Unlike the strong Nelson proposal which provided for independent testing to prove the safety of additives, the FDA would only require the manufacturer to supply data showing his product to be safe.

The potential of a real double-edged sword exists here as far as the consumer is concerned. It the antibiotics are by and large removed from the animals' feed, the animals will be relatively smaller, forcing meat prices higher. If the antibiotics are certified safe by the FDA, by whatever nebulous testing data, the whole affair could turn out as the cyclamate controversy did. For the original cyclamate research by the manufacturer was rejected by the FDA, but then in a switch approved, using the FDA's own insufficient tests.

A meat lobby spokesman said that to his knowledge no disease had ever come from treated animal feed. Indeed, it might be a hard thing to prove, for it's not quite as easy as diagnosing a common cold. And finally, there are the drug manufacturers—the antibiotics for feed run into millions of dollars annually. What chance does the consumer have if one $4,500-a-year Nader's Raider has to take on the cattle, pharmaceutical companies, and the FDA—at once?

In January of 1950 Abbott Laboratories applied to have a new product called Sucaryl Sodium, which is a cyclamate derivative, approved. The company stated that the product was for those who were forced to restrict their intake of sugar. The FDA threw out the test data submitted with the application, saying that it was worthless and was a perfect example of how not to go about proving a substance was safe. However, the FDA took the unusual step of approving the product on the basis of tests it had conducted in its own labs. It was later shown that the FDA's own data revealed an appallingly high incidence of malignant tumors in the animals tested, but that this was either ignored or misunderstood.

The case was just beginning. The Food Nutrition Board of the National Academy of Sciences-National Research Council warned the FDA about cyclamates in 1954, 1955, 1962, and again in 1968. But by 1968 the cyclamate industry had become a billion dollar business and was not about to fold just because a few customers suffered diarrhea from excessive cyclamate ingestion.

In 1966 a Japanese experiment showed that cyclamates in the body are converted into cyclohexylamine (CHA). CHA is very toxic; it speeds heart action, raises blood pressure, and can interfere with the action of other drugs. In animals it has been shown to produce a large number of stillborn young, causing chromosome damage and a multitude of birth defects.

An FDA biochemist named Jacqueline Verrett told the FDA of the effects of cyclamates at a seminar in March, 1968, and she reiterated her contention that the substance was capable of producing adnormal chicken embryos in her year-end report in December of 1968.

Another FDA investigator, Dr. Marvin Legator, found chromosome damage in his animal studies with cyclamates. His findings became public in December of 1968. Dr. Legator sent a memo of his findings to assistant FDA Commissioner Daniel Banes, describing the tests and urging that "The use of cyclamates should be immediately curtailed, pending the outcome of additional studies."

While finding its way to the top of the FDA, Dr. Legator's summarized conclusion was deleted, but his research, still carrying his name, was passed along. His findings finally appeared in *Science,* September 21, 1969, and were quickly picked up by *Newsweek.* A network newsman saw the *Newsweek* story and contacted the FDA, which in turn put him in touch with Jacqueline Verrett. When Dr. Verrett told the nation her story, the gig was all over for the drug companies.

HEW, looking to save face, turned to Abbott. Abbott had a test group of animals going. They were ordered to slaughter and autopsy, and to no one's surprise, some of the rats had bladder tumors.

Finch had no choice; he had to ban cyclamates, but when he appeared before the press, he was somewhat less than candid. He claimed his action was required by law and he totally neglected to mention the twenty-year heritage of the product he was banning. Indeed, it was painful for the producers of cyclamate products to have to scrap their stocks, but no one will ever know, definitely, what effect it had on the American public. The National Institute of Cancer reported that bladder cancer doubled between 1945 and 1965. It may be another generation before the full effects are felt, because this particular type of cancer usually takes ten years at least and more often twenty before it develops.

The consumer still got the shaft. Diet and soft drinks had to come off the shelves by January 1, 1970. However, under pressure from the canners, a February 1, 1970, deadline was moved back to September 1, to let them squeeze in one more canning season.

In February, 1970, Finch said cyclamates could be

used as non-prescription drugs added to foods if they were labeled as such. But on August 14, 1970, the FDA announced its intention to make the across-the-board ban stick.

It's even more interesting what a couple of companies did with their "overstock" of cyclamates. After all, consumers are consumers. One company sent its diet liquid to Laos. Another put hundreds of cases into prisons and mental hospitals in Ohio, where it was accepted with thanks.

But manufacturers of cyclamates may have the last laugh. A bill passed by a House Judiciary Subcommittee would reimburse the manufacturer for their losses suffered in the wake of the ban. According to a member of the subcommittee's staff, this would be between one hundred-one hundred-twenty million dollars—with the tab being picked up by the consumer—the taxpayers. According to the *Wall Street Journal,* the Nixon administration is lending its assets to the bill by not opposing it.

Under the terms of the bill, any manufacturer pressing a claim would have to demonstrate his losses occurred from "good-faith reliance" on cyclamate use since it was on the FDA's GRAS list prior to the ban. Many California congressmen were said to be most anxious to see the bill passed because one cooperative in that state was readying a fifteen million-dollar claim. The bill's chief sponsor was Representative B. F. Sisk (D-Cal).

The bill's chances were rated as good—if consumer groups did not oppose it.

One of the most flagrant examples of the FDA's failure to act in the public interest concerns a substance consumed by millions of Americans daily.

On January 28, 1972, the FDA took saccharin off its Generally Recognized As Safe (GRAS) list and placed specific limits on its use. Charles C. Edwards, FDA Commissioner, said he took the action because bladder tumors had been found in rats which had been fed large doses of saccharin. If the tumors prove cancerous, then saccharin will have to come off the market altogether, even though it has been acceptable for over eighty years. The limit set by the FDA, one gram per adult per day, would mean that you would have to take sixty saccharin tablets daily or drink more than a six-pack of diet soft drink daily.

Saccharin has been the main sugar substitute since cyclamates were banned on October 18, 1969, by then HEW Secretary Robert Finch. Ralph Nader's Study Group Report on the Food and Drug Administration called *The Chemical Feast* documents the twenty-year horror to get cyclamates off the public marketplace. One wonders how long the public will have to wait for a verdict on saccharin, which has been around since the nineteenth century and is the staple of more than one producer.

A trio of FDA scientists said in 1951 that saccharin in particularly large amounts might be cancer-inducing. The Nader Task Group study said that the FDA's actions on such preliminary findings—which would not be considered too far out of the ordinary—should be to follow up. But the FDA did nothing of the sort. A 1968 report on the substance referred to the seventeen-year-old 1951 study, but said: "In view of the small number of tumors this incidence cannot be considered significant without additional experiments." One would think that over a seventeen-year period, the FDA would have conducted some additional experiments.

The government actually had reservations over the effects of saccharin for over sixty years, but no less a personage than President Theodore Roosevelt, siding with the powerful industry, railed: "anybody who says saccharin is injurious is an idiot. Dr. Rixby gives it to me every day." Yet for all the doubts the FDA and government agencies of the early 1900s had about the safety of saccharin, the substance continued to be listed as safe.

Another study, the results of which were released in 1969 caused the FDA to take another look at saccharin. The study was conducted by Dr. George Bryan of the University of Wisconsin, and it found that a mixture of cholesterol and saccharin caused bladder cancer in mice. In a control group of 106 mice treated only with cholesterol, thirteen contracted cancer.

The second look began early in 1970, and on January 28, 1972, after protracted stalling the FDA did remove saccharin from the GRAS list pending the outcome of a definitive set of research studies. Interim limits for use of the drug were established—one gram a day per adult. To reach this level one would have to consume more than a six-pack of typical diet soda or take some sixty saccharin tablets with his coffee.

The order required that beverages, foods and food mixes containing saccharin list it as such on their labels. Reportedly the action was the first step in a close look at all 600 items on the GRAS list.

Another of the FDA's mis-actions was the Great Cola Caper. On January 21, 1966, after nearly thirty years of trying, the cola drink makers of America won what could be construed as their greatest victory—a labeling hoax so devious that unravelling all the pieces is still difficult.

Consumers who are interested in knowing what is in the beverages they consume will find no satisfaction from the soft drink industry. The main issue at stake was acknowledging the content of caffeine. The manufacturers were reluctant to indicate on the label that caffeine was part of their beverage. For years and years they had successfully stalled requirements which would have made such labeling mandatory.

The way the industry circumvented the problem is almost too incredible to believe: the industry had the FDA make caffeine a mandatory element of cola drinks. If an element is required by law in a beverage, then it does not have to be explicitly stated on the label that the product contains that particular ingredient. In fact, the law was broadened to include pepper drinks, which also include caffeine. How many "pepper" drinks do you know of? There's only one major one and the loophole was made to accommodate it.

The FDA's action in this instance is shameful and a blatant disregard for the health of the consumer.

Caffeine is a mild stimulant. Some religious groups like the Mormons reject its use by their practitioners. Physicians have found it a contributing factor to heart attacks. That the FDA could resort to such a transparent ruse is incredible. A survey taken by the FDA in the mid-sixties showed some cola beverages did not contain caffeine or contained it only in minute amounts, so those bottlers who wanted to call their product a cola now had to add caffeine, a consumer health risk. The FDA approved the no-label standard over scores of consumer complaints.

The way the FDA laws are written, the industry has a field day. There's the new product category. If you can't make it as a mayonnaise you can be a "salad dressing." When Gatorade was put on the market, it was not a soft drink. It was by definition a "thirst quencher." What does a thirst quencher have as its ingredients? Anything the manufacturer wants it to have.

Who loses in this calculated assault? Not the companies who take their vaguely labeled products to the consumer. Just the consumer.

Another Nader target has been the baby food manufacturers. They have added unconscionable amounts of starch and salt to their products in an effort to make it taste good for mother. Why not? Mother buys their product, not baby.

Monosodium glutamate is one of the chemicals added to baby food to make it more palatable. Ralph Nader was in the forefront of those who wanted it out of baby food and off the GRAS list. On October 24, 1969, the three largest baby food manufacturers—Gerber, Beech-Nut and Heinz, decided to voluntarily eliminate MSG from their products. Mind you, there was nothing wrong with MSG. Just consider it a "goodwill" gesture by the industry.

Like cyclamates, the problem did not spring full-born overnight. In 1957 a scientist reported damage to the retinas of new born animals which he believed was caused by MSG. However, the crusader with the white hat in this whole episode was Dr. John Olney of the Washington University School of Medicine in St. Louis. He found that injecting MSG into infant mice caused brain damage. He testified about his findings before the Senate Select Committee on Food, Nutrition and Health headed by Senator George McGovern in July of 1969.

McGovern queried the FDA on the matter and was assured by Commissioner Herbert Ley there were at least four tests which showed MSG to be perfectly safe. In fact, this was not the case. At least two of the tests had not been completed. (One was being conducted by Dr. Jacqueline Verrett who played such a crucial role in the cyclamate controversy.)

James Turner went after all four tests. Turner and his associates found many errors causing Commissioner Ley to issue "clarifications" to the McGovern committee on his statements about the Olney tests. On the other tests he was silent. Outside analysis pointed to the fact that two of the tests were preliminary, a third had not been conducted and yet another was not even an FDA test. Ley finally backed down on all four tests.

Science News hit the FDA buckpassing. Olney wrote *Science News* saying they had been too kind to the Commissioner and his associates.

What was even more incredible was an attack on Olney by Dan Gerber of the baby food company. He acknowledged the existence of the tests but damned them because unnamed scientists disagreed with the conclusion. Gerber went on to castigate Nader: "A considerable amount of publicity was generated from this testimony [Olney before the McGovern committee]. This publicity has been kept alive by continuous television appearances of one of the principal consumer protection crusaders, Ralph Nader . . ." Yet five months later, in the face of such unwanted publicity the companies withdrew their products "voluntarily from the marketplace.

The studies have shown that there is a likely possibility that MSG is a teratogen, a substance different from a carcinogen (a substance capable of inducing cancer) or a mutagen (a substance capable of altering a family's genetic history). A teratogen causes abnormal development in the fertilized egg of an animal after it's begun to divide and grow in the embryo stage. It is capable of damaging only that offspring and not subsequent ones like a mutagen.

In the face of such a threat the baby food companies retreated. Nader found, however, that as late as the fall of 1970, over a year later, it was still possible to buy baby food with MSG in it. He queried the Gerber Company which replied: "We agreed not to manufacture baby food with MSG anymore, but we didn't agree to take what we had made off the shelves or out of the warehouses." The company further said that in some of the smaller stores the product would have a shelf life of two years or more.

Nader is still less than sanguine about the prospects for genuine reform in the baby food industry. He says the companies are marketing fancier food with less nutritional value per dollar.

The 1967 Meat Inspection Act is a singular tribute to Nader's unflinching efforts in the consumer's behalf. Veteran Capitol Hill watchers felt that the time was not right for a strong bill which would cost the meat interests millions of dollars. Nader felt otherwise.

Nader's initial volley in the fight took the form of an article in the *New Republic* in July 1967. The article was called: "We're Still in the Jungle." In it Nader described the experiences of a Congressman from Iowa who had previously been a farmer. This farmer turned Congressman had been to meat auctions where the interest was largely with the diseased and maimed specimens rather than the healthy ones. Of course, these animals were cheaper and, as it turned out, more profitable. They were headed for intrastate slaughterhouses, not under Federal jurisdiction.

The Congressman, Neil Smith of Iowa, had been trying since 1961 to get a tough meat bill through the house, but until 1967 had little success. Smith's amendments to the Meat Inspection Act (which had been passed in 1906 after the publication of Upton Sinclair's muckraking work *The Jungle* and had not been substantially changed since that time) would have extended the Federal province to intrastate slaughterhouses as well.

(Nader himself, though not a conspicuous consumer by any means, is known to like a good slab of prime ribs, done medium—but only if Federally inspected.)

In unregulated plants, a variety of abuses were common. The number of 4-D (dead, diseased, dying, disabled) animals was large. Conditions for meat preparation were often unsanitary. It was easy to conceal the real character of the meat with additives like sulfites, antibiotics like Aureomycin, and detergents.

It was Nader's contention that fifteen percent of the commercially slaughtered animals (about nineteen million head by his count) and about twenty-five percent of all commercially processed meats (enough to feed about fifteen percent of the U.S. population) were not covered by Federal laws. Nader said that Federal inspectors had ferreted out some twenty-two million pounds of contaminated meat. He further contended that contaminated horsemeat and meat from diseased animals intended for pet food ended up in hamburger and processed luncheon meats. Baloney and hot dogs were the recipients of among other things, eyeballs, lungs, hog blood, chopped hide, and other supposedly unusable carcass parts.

A report was prepared by the Department of Agriculture in 1963, but only part of it was made public. According to Nader, the more revolting parts were never put on the table for public consumption because the details were too critical of meat-packing practices.

Even those portions of the report made available had little impact. Forty-one states had meat inspection laws, some quite weak. Only twenty-six provided for mandatory inspection before slaughter, the others were purely voluntary. Only twenty-five states had statutes providing for inspection of processed meat food products. Nader charged that the Department of Agriculture was in bed with the meat packers because it would do nothing to effectively toughen the packing and slaughtering conditions. "Despite the devastating evidence in its files," he said, "the U.S. Department of Agriculture adheres in its policymaking to the avoidance of unfavorable publicity about meat products as the first priority. Consequently, years have passed without Congressional hearings, when all the department had to do was request them."

The initial bill that the Subcommittee drafted was sneered at by Nader. The bill provided in essence that the Federal government would give the states technical and financial assistance if they would toughen their laws. If they didn't there was nothing the federal government could do. Some regulatory power!

Nader saw on the horizon the National Association of State Agricultural Departments and the Meat Packers Association, a trade group, waiting for a chance to deliver fatal blows to the already weak bill. What was even worse, the Department of Agriculture was opting to take some of the FDA's regulatory power in the inspection of meat. He felt the Department should not take on the added responsibilities because of the poor job it had done in administering the regulatory provisions of the 1957 Poultry Products Inspection Act.

Nader told a *Playboy* interviewer that the meat packers had strong allies in the Department of Agriculture because the Department was concerned with stimulating the economy "by promoting meat sales and fear that any bad publicity would hurt business . . . The Department's promotional and regulatory roles frequently clash—but the regulatory always seems to come out on the short end." Nader saw the attempt of the Department of Agriculture to take over the meat inspection system as a step that would cripple the existent Federal system, a workable if overworked bureaucratic arm.

In an attempt to raise public consciousness of what was going on Nader made a ten city tour. He went from Boston to Los Angeles, making extensive use of the airwaves, to get his point across. The result was a flood of mail against the pending bill to Betty Furness, then the President's consumer advisor. Miss Furness told *Newsweek:* "You wouldn't believe the letters, they were from meat inspectors themselves, their wives, ordinary consumers—everybody—demanding tough action."

Nader went before the Subcommittee as a witness, pounding all his facts home. He told the committee members that if 100-200 million dollars could be spent annually on highways then certainly forty-five million dollars could be set aside for meat inspection.

In a *New Republic* article called "Watch That Hamburger" he described the subcommittee proceedings as industry apologists tried to befuddle, obfuscate, and minimize the issues at hand. The president of the Western States Meat Packers Association, commented that Americans bought their meat knowing "that it is the safest, cleanest and most wholesome in the entire world." Nader quoted Aled P. Davies, vice president of the American Meat Institute as saying that state inspection programs "have provided the kind of consumer protection in the various states that the people in those states thought necessary and been willing to pay for." A rather cavalier attitude, to say the least.

Nader visualized a kind of Gresham's law at work here where 4D or bad meat had a competitive advantage over healthy meat. With the enormous profits in the balance, a businessman looking at his profit and loss sheet could not be tempted to remain for long on the wholesome side of the street, especially when his chances of getting caught were nil, and even if he were caught and disciplined the penalty would still be cheaper than the profits that would be lost.

As always, Nader articulately cleared things up. He saw three areas where pressure should be applied to the meat processors: on their selection of animals, on the slaughtering conditions, and on additives or preservatives. He chided Betty Furness for not responding to his letter asking where she stood. He went after individual Senators and Congressmen challenging their consciences.

Nader's pressure on the Senate resulted in the passage of a tough meat control law by a vote of 89–2, which was signed into effect by President Lyndon Johnson on December 6, 1967 as Nader, Miss Furness and the aged Upton Sinclair watched.

Said one Senate pundit: "The meat bill was Ralph's finest hour." Hundreds of processing plants were closed either permanently or pending upgrading conditions. The law provided that the state be given two years to upgrade plants in its jurisdiction or face Federal takeover. By mid-'71 forty-four states had equalled the Federal standards; the six that hadn't were placed under Federal supervision.

Much is still left to be done. Nader says that thirty-five million dollars or roughly one-third the cost of an atomic submarine would give us an adequate inspection system. As for himself, he muses: "I would personally never eat a hamburger, a hot dog, a sausage, or any luncheon meat; it's not beyond the realm of possibility you could get a good hamburger, hot dog or sausage, but why take a chance?"

A study published in the 1972 issue of *Consumer Reports* considered frankfurters in some fourteen cities. CU found the old American standby to be wanting, at least by its former standards. In 1937 the Department of Agriculture found that frankfurters averaged some 19.6 percent protein. Those in the CU test, a wide sample, showed a disappointing 11.7 percent. The frank of thirty-five years ago contained nineteen percent fat on the average versus today's 28 percent.

Among the additives—which are permissible under law—that were found by CU: corn syrup, dextrose, salt, spices, spice oils, MSG; and such color fixtures as sodium erythorbate, sodium ascorbate, ascorbic acid, citric acid, sodium nitrate, and sodium nitrite.

The latter two are of grave concern to food technologists and research scientists. Their safety beyond a doubt has not been proven. In large doses nitrites can be poisonous. They are also suspected of contributing to a substance that may cause cancer and genetic damage. The nitrites combine with amines to form nitrosamines. They have caused cancers in a variety of laboratory animals.

Both FDA Commissioner Charles C. Edwards and Dr. Virgil Wodicka, head of the FDA's Bureau of Foods have admitted that the nitrites might have something to do with the formation of cancers. Under the Delaney Amendment of 1958 the FDA has the power to ban the substances until they have been proven safe. But since the food industry has millions of dollars at stake and the development of an alternate fixer would involve time and money, the FDA has decided in concert with the food interests that burying its head is the best answer.

Lack of enough protein, excessive fat, (CU thinks twenty-five percent to be quite generous), adulterants and additives are not the only problem. CU found an excessive amount of bacteria in the samples which could be caused at the initial processing point or anywhere between the time the hot dog leaves the plant and reaches the consumer. Also, some nineteen percent of the samples had insect and rodent contamination. Better plant sanitation and quality control in processing were just two of CU's recommendations to the hot dog makers.

The hot dog industry did not take to the CU study. "It's surprising to us," said Dr. W.J. Aunan of the American Meat Institute, "when they report that more than forty percent of their samples had begun to spoil. We can't help but wonder where they obtained them and how the samples were handled prior to testing."

Aunan said he saw nothing wrong with using nitrites since they inhibit bacterial growth. He was less sanguine about examining the contentions that they cause cancer. Aunan further said that the CU study was "an inaccurate, misleading and biased attack on one of the nation's most popular foods."

When reporters queried the FDA in the wake of the CU report, they were told that an interdepartmental report on nitrates—a joint effort of the Agriculture Department, the National Cancer Institute and the FDA—was in the works.

New York City's Commissioner of Consumer Affairs Bess Myerson joined the fray on the side of CU and Nader. She commented: "After I found out what was in hot dogs, I stopped eating them." When asked if she were recommending that consumers not eat hot dogs, she replied: "I am suggesting that the consumer make up his own mind. We are going to the FDA to see that the consumer is protected. It is time to stand up against the degradation of our food supply." She also went after the Department of Agriculture, which recommended that the use of sodium acid pyrophosphate (SAPP) which helps speed up the "fixing" or coloring of hot dogs, be continued.

SAPP has been used for a number of years in bacon, ham and other products. Harrison Wellford, a senior Nader associate who wrote a critical study on the Department of Agriculture and is Nader's meat expert, decided not to oppose SAPP. He feels that nitrates and nitrites are much more important issues. However, when the Agriculture Department indicated it was going to side with the pro-SAPP forces, it received a spate of anti-SAPP letters from irate consumers.

With a half-pound of SAPP sprinkled into every 100 pounds of frankfurter stuffing, production time would be cut in half, a considerable saving for the manufacturer.

The *Wall Street Journal* reported that 350 anti-SAPP letters had been received by the Department of Agriculture versus some fifty favorable industry opinions. Under the broad provisions of the 1967 Wholesome Meat Act the Department can zap SAPP. But only time will tell if the undernourished hot dog will get yet another additive.

Nader and CU have been most vocal on another popular diet staple—hamburger. Nader has said there's a possibility of getting a safe hamburger but he wouldn't chance it. A CU study in late 1971 showed many areas where the processors and sellers could improve the quality of the product they were hawking. Big supermarkets pose a problem. They are exempt from routine supervision under the provisions of the Federal Meat Inspection Act and the Wholesome Meat Act.

About twenty percent of 126 samples purchased had begun to spoil when CU got them. Only twenty-seven percent of the samples purchased in Philadelphia, where the majority of the survey took place, passed muster on coliform count, the amount of fecal contamination present. Some hamburger purchased in Los Angeles, although bacteriologically better, had insect parts and rodent hair.

The Federal Government has set a thirty percent fat limit in ground beef. CU feels that twenty-five percent is plenty. Most of the survey's samples made the thirty percent limit.

CU feels that under the 1967 Wholesome Meat Act the Agriculture Department has the power to set and enforce bacteriological standards—which do not currently exist. CU also felt that that spot-checking of retail establishments should also be encouraged. One practice that CU would like to see stopped is an Agriculture Department rule which allows restaurant suppliers to water their hamburger from two to ten percent, ostensibly to improve palatability. Without knowing it, the consumer is paying for the water in his hamburger.

Harrison Wellford, one of Nader's senior associates at the Center for the Study of Responsive Law, monitors the meat industry. He was the author of the report and the head of the research team that produced *Sowing the Wind: Meat, Pesticides, and the Public Interest.*

Some of the report's assertions such as government favoring business interests over those of the consumer had been made previously in other Nader tomes. And that legislation passed in consumer interests such as the 1967 Wholesome Meat Act, a major Nader victory, is being indifferently enforced. It further concluded: "An act which originally promised to extend uniform Federal standards to the twenty-five percent of meat not processed under Federal control in 1967 may result in all meat being processed in fifty separate state-controlled systems."

The Federal system of only visibly inspecting meat for defects came under attack. The report said that regular micro-biological monitoring should take place.

Pesticide abuse also came in for strong criticism. The report held that responsible use of pesticides is proper but that often corporate interests do not fully inform individual farmers of the dangers of overusage.

Wellford and Peter Shuck, another Nader's Raider, are editors of *The Consumer Protection Report,* which they began issuing from the Center for the Study of Responsive Law in December, 1971. The newsletter, the editors hoped, would become a sort of hot line for federal and state meat and poultry inspectors. And indeed by the second issue there were some hair-raising stories, both signed and unsigned, of various inspectors' exploits combatting the meat industry.

Among the topics included in the first few issues of the newsletter were: threats against meat inspectors; a successful Nader suit to release data about the consumer protection activities of the Department of Agriculture under the Freedom of Information Act; the great danger of using PCBs (polychlorinated biphenyls) in food packaging; and the use of nitrates and nitrites in hot dogs and sausages.

As scared consumers turned to brain food or fish, Nader let another shocking salvo fly. He claimed that 2,200 fish processing plants were inspected less than once a year and virtually no fishing boats at all were checked. He said that deterioration, lack of adequate sanitation in processing plants, taking tainted fish from the waters, and the ever-present danger of additives to make bad fish resemble good, plagued the fishing industry. Fish processing plants have problems resembling those of meat packers. Implements and tables were not clean and were encrusted with pieces of rotted fish flesh.

The fishing boats were a major problem as Nader saw it. Most were distressingly old and did not have proper refrigeration facilities. The fish would be held in the hold for one to two weeks with only a few blocks of ice to refrigerate them. Nader said that fish stored above zero degrees begin to deteriorate.

On one holiday weekend in 1966 some 400 people suffered salmonella poisoning in New York City. In 1963 nine people died from botulism poisoning after consuming improperly canned tuna. A huge FDA recall of canned salmon took place in 1967 when several cans were found to have unsealed seams.

Nader quoted an MIT professor who had reportedly been told by a fishery owner that he "could make just as much money selling bad fish as he could selling good fish."

The housewife goes into the store and picks up a large can which has a half-dozen oranges staring at her on the label. It may be orange juice, watered orange juice, orangeade, orange blend, orange concentarate, or orange drink. This has long been a pet crusade of both Nader and New York City Consumer Affairs Commissioner, Bess Myerson. Nader was once surprised by receiving fresh orange juice on a plane and clipped the label to write and thank the manufacturer.

"It's a crime to sneak water into whiskey," Miss Myerson had said. "Orange juice needs and deserves the same protection." Miss Myerson wanted mandatory labeling calling all 100 percent orange juice drinks "orange juice, orangeade, orange blend, orange concentrate, or from fifty to ninety-nine percent she wanted labeled "orange dilute." Those with percentages from five to forty-nine would be known as "orange water" and those with less than five percent could not use "orange" at all.

The FDA's standards tended more toward the industry side of the coin and were not as revealing or as drastic as those proposed by Miss Myerson. One hundred percent orange juice can call itself precisely that. If the product contains seventy to ninety-five percent orange juice, it will be called "orange juice blend." From thirty-five to seventy percent will be known as "orange drink" and ten to thirty percent "orange-flavored drink." The recommendations are helpful only if the consumer sets out to memorize the cutoff figures. The FDA should require the exact percentage to accompany the nomenclature.

Most of the loaves of white bread consumed in this country are made up of an outstanding component—air. Anything that adds more nutrients or seemingly beneficial substances would seem like a good idea, right? Almost.

Many women and children suffer from iron deficiency anemia, which results in poor appetite and a tendency to tire quickly while working at a particular task. It would almost seem logical to help correct this by supplying more iron in a common foodstuff—bread. The view is pronounced by the Council on Foods and Nutrition of the AMA. Nader and his raiders doubtless were surprised when the proposed increase from eight to twelve milligrams per pound to about twenty-five was sharply criticized by a number of prominent physicians.

The FDA was caught squarely in the middle. There were experts on both sides and it seemed no matter which decision the FDA came to, it would displease a portion of the scientific community.

Dr. Jean Mayer of Harvard, who chaired the 1970 White House Conference on Food, questioned whether menstruating women would get enough iron even with the enriched bread. He was upset because another prevailing myth might have gotten a chance to circulate: eat enough bread and you've taken care of your iron requirement.

Dr. William H. Crosby, Jr., hematology chief at New England Medical Center, had a much more substantial objection. He claimed that the added iron could be fatal to those with rare blood conditions. Sickle cell anemia and hemochromatosis, a disease characterized by large deposits of iron stored in the body, were just two of the conditions he mentioned. The added iron could be stored in the liver, pancreas, testicles, bone marrow and heart muscles; liver sclerosis, diabetes, sterility and heart disease were some of the conditions that might be caused.

In all, more than 100 physicians and scientists sent letters of protest over the new standards to the FDA. In response, the FDA held off their implementation. No decision was expected on the matter before May 1, 1972 at the earliest. The response to the FDA standards was precisely the type of citizen-consumer response from professionals that, from the outset of his operations, Nader had tried to encourage.

Nader has long attacked the impurity of meat and the adulteration of packaged products, so it came as little surprise when in early 1972 the FDA disclosed it would soon make public a list of filth tolerances allowed in certain foods. Commented an FDA official: "There are insect fragments in every loaf of bread," adding that 100 percent pure loaf was impossible.

The list which the FDA has slugged: "Administrative Guidelines on Unavoidable Defects in Food for Human Use" has some 100 consumer items on it. Among the less savory substances which are likely to find their way, cleverly camouflaged, onto your table are: wood shavings, pebbles, and rat excreta.

For instance, less than two percent filth allowance in canned apricots is acceptable. The Pure Food and Drug Act provides for no such allowance, however, stating: "Food shall be deemed to be adulterated if it consists in whole or in part of any filthy, putrid or decomposed substance."

Spices, in particular, are thought to have large amounts of contaminants in them. The FDA had been reluctant to publish the guidelines because they feared consumers would become angered when they saw that one rodent pellet per product is acceptable but two are not. The spice industry knew the level as did the American Spice Trade Association, but consumers did not.

Scientists are outraged that filth is tolerated in spices at all. Dr. Clyde Christensen of the University of Minnesota, a student of fungal diseases, rejects the assumption that no filth should add to the cost of spices. The current FDA guidelines permit filth "as the lowest amount that can be permitted under good production procedure." The FDA pretends it will reduce filth tolerance as technology becomes more advanced.

On March 28, 1972, the FDA released its filth limits on seventy-nine items including chocolate (limit: 150 insect fragments and four rodent hairs per 225 grams), tomato juice (ten fruit fly eggs per 100 grams), tomato soup (microscopic mold in no more than forty percent of samples), peanut butter (fifty insect fragments per

100 grams), and corn meal (no more than five rodent pellets in one-fifth of the sub-samples).

The limits have been kept secret since the list was instituted in 1911. Some of the limits have been decreased since then due to better food technology.

James Turner, author of *The Chemical Feast* and former Nader associate, said of the list: "As things currently stand, industry doesn't find it possible to eliminate these things but if the pressure were put on they would find ways to eliminate them."

But Dr. Virgil O. Wodicka, Director of the FDA Bureau of Foods, disagreed. If food was required to be totally pure, he said "there would be no food sold in the United States."

It's hard to imagine Ralph Nader going home for the evening, turning on his color television set (sitting, of course, the required six feet away), tugging on a pair of slippers, and reading through the evening paper, all the while puffing on a huge black stogie. Nader has said that diatomaceous earth, rock wool, glass fibers and maybe asbestos may be contained in cigars, cigarillos, and cigarettes. Nader warned that these additives could prove toxic to the individual who smoked them.

The investigation began when an organic chemist, Dr. Albert J. Fritsch, and an associate at the Center for the Study of Responsive Law checked U. S. Patent Office files and ascertained that the tobacco industry was using additives in reconstituted tobacco. The reconstituted tobacco, which is composed of stems and previously wasted products, is used as cigar wrappers or added to cigar fillers. Nader said one purpose of the additives, according to the patent literature, was to firm the cigar ash.

The American Cancer Society and the Environmental Sciences Laboratory of Mount Sinai Hospital in New York City are studying the additives. Nader asked the FTC to see if any laws under its jurisdiction had been violated. And the Senate Commerce Committee pondered asking the FDA if it should require removal of the tobacco product under the Hazardous Substances Act.

Yes, what this country needs is a *safe* five cent cigar.

On November 28, 1971, Ralph Nader and an associate, Dr. Sidney Wolfe, wrote to FDA Commissioner Charles Edwards and asked him to remove from the marketplace all products containing hexachlorophene that were not prescribed by a doctor. The pair also asked the FDA to place restrictions on its medical use.

Wolfe and Nader cited studies which showed that the use of products containing hexachlorophene can sometimes raise the level of hexachlorophene in the blood near levels which have cause brain damage in research animals. Wolfe did concede that hexachlorophene can be useful in fighting infection, but only under tightly controlled medical supervision.

Wolfe and Nader are not the only ones concerned about the problem. A large number of dermatologists have become alarmed at the proliferation of aerosol products that contain the chemical, including underarm deodorants, vaginal sprays, and foot sprays. Soaps like the popular Phisohex also have hexachlorophene present as a constituent element. "Hexachlorophene is finding its way into a growing number of products," said Dr. Wolfe. "Anybody who uses several products, each with a small amount of hexachlorophene, could wind up with large concentrations of the chemical."

A spokesman for the Cosmetic, Toiletry and Fragrance Association said that banning hexachlorophene from all products which now contained it would be a severe action. He did concede, however, that infants and burn victims were more likely to be susceptible to the less pleasant effects of the chemical. Other industry sources were similarly unmoved. Said Johnson and Johnson: "Hexachlorophene is used because we consider it to be an effective anti-bacterial agent." Gillette's response was: "To date there seems to be no evidence that the chemical is a hazard in the small amounts found in our products."

So at the moment the consumer has a stand-off. He knows that hexachlorophene may be a problem and he should be able to avoid those products which contain it by reading the labels. Not so. Secret spray deodorant and Ban spray both list hexachlorophene as an element, but the popular Right Guard does not. When one consumer reporter queried the company why this was so, he got this response: "The information is not listed for competitive reasons. It's not required by any government agency. And it wouldn't do anybody any good." The spokesman did concede that the product contained hexachlorophene as do, he asserted, "all major brands of deodorant." Why not clearly label it as such, then? One popular brand-name vaginal spray, Vespre, said it contained hexachlorophene; another, Brand X, packaged by a local chain under the store's name, did not. A can of Dr. Scholl's foot powder had hexachlorophene clearly labeled, another name brand did not. "Show us where we have to label it in the public interest," said a member of their corporate public relations staff, "prove to me that it's dangerous."

In March of 1971, the FDA indicated it would soon decide whether hexachlorophene should be banned outright from commercial soaps. An FDA scientist stated that hexachlorophene would be a problem if used on burned or broken skin and then washed off. Ostensibly to protect the consumer, the FDA said it was pondering three courses of action: (1) restrain the amount of hexachlorophene in products, (2) require a warning label and (3) ban the substance from any product except prescription items.

On January 5, 1972, the FDA issued hexachlorophene use guidelines in response to Nader's pressure. The agency prefaced its remarks with a statement that it had not been proven that hexachlorophene caused harm to humans, used under normal conditions.

But more significantly the agency noted: ". . . animal studies and abnormal human use have shown toxicity; repeated daily use of drug and cosmetic products containing hexachlorophene has resulted in sufficient human blood hexachlorophene levels, and the margin of safety between present human exposure and the threshold toxicity level is uncertain."

The proposed action banned hexachlorophene from cosmetic products until further studies were completed.

It would be available as a prescription item and over the counter in some non-cosmetic products.

The FDA said that all skin-cleaning products containing more than three-fourths of one percent of hexachlorophene would be restricted to prescription and hospital use. Products that had less than this amount would be forced to carry a warning label that stated the product contained hexachlorophene, was for external use only, and that the treated surface be washed thoroughly. Only those cosmetics which needed a small amount of hexachlorophene as a preservative were exempted.

Manufacturers were given sixty days to appeal the FDA's ruling. Some 300 to 500 products containing the chemical in varying amounts: after-shave lotions, shaving creams, medicated shampoos, soaps, foot powders and the whole realm of spray deodorants. The reaction was sure to be great.

Even now the effectiveness of hexachlorophene for acne and other uses has been questioned in experimental studies. The National Academy of Sciences said that three percent hexachlorophene solutions are only possibly effective in treating staph skin infections and acne. The substance was found to be lacking in efficacy as a vaginal douche, for treatment of eczema or scaling, and in treating wounds and burns.

Many of the manufacturers are claiming that their product contains far less than the three percent considered by the FDA as extremely dangerous. But the spray products leave this open to question. When the vaporized propellant evaporates on the skin, the residue of hexachlorophene can be much higher than indicated on the can.

The only way to ascertain how much hexachlorophene a product contains now is to write to the manufacturer. If all the FDA edicts stick, that will no longer be necessary, thanks to Ralph Nader and Dr. Sidney Wolfe.

It began when Nader, the omnivorous reader and sometimes silent monitor or consumer interests in the strangest places, came across a technical paper early in

1967 by Dr. Karl Z. Morgan, who was director of health physics at the Oak Ridge National Laboratory and an acknowledged expert in the X-ray field. The paper cautioned against overexposing medical patients to X-rays during their treatment.

Nader began corresponding with Dr. Morgan, who proved to be just the tip of the iceberg. He then compiled a great amount of research data (much of it from state and federal files) and talked to other health physicists and radiologists.

Morgan estimated that there were 3,600 deaths each year caused by X-radiation and "probably thousands of injuries for every death." Dr. Morgan went on to add that "no matter how great the medical benefits derived from X-rays, there is no justification of the fact that because of poor techniques with obsolete and improperly operated equipment, many X-ray exposures are ten or more times that needed for best diagnostic results."

One of the more spectacular aspects to emerge was the fact that an expectant mother over-exposed to such X-rays could suffer a miscarriage, or at the extreme, produce a deformed offspring.

Nader's figures showed that the possibility could be a reality just in terms of sheer numbers. In 1966, he claimed, 150 million X-rays and seven million fluoroscope films were made in this country. The fluoroscope may be especially dangerous because its radiation can be 100 to 200 times that of a normal X-ray.

Part of the problem Nader attributes to a swing in the scientific concensus about the nature of radiation. Now we know that excessive radiation can cause serious eye problems, forms of neoplastic disease (cancer), and simpler and more common things like loss of hair. One study has indicated, according to Nader, that the rate of thyroid cancer has grown from two percent in the 1920's to fifteen percent for a comparable span at mid-century. Nader points out that X-rays were used to treat a variety of common ailments like acne until well into the 1950's.

Genetic mutation, because of large amounts of radiation, is also a distinct possibility. A man could receive a dose of 100 times that from radioactive fallout during one medical diagnosis. The pregnant woman could suffer distinct injury to her child.

Nader, upon Dr. Morgan's advice, made public a list of sixty-five steps that might be taken by the average doctor or dentist to reduce radiation: for instance, the use of fast vs. slow film. The fast film costs a bit more and the X-ray machine must be slightly modified. However, the X-ray dosage goes down considerably if these two things are taken care of. Also, better shielding, both for the patient and for those who are forced to work in the surroundings where X-rays are constantly being emitted. Again this costs a few dollars but in the long run would certainly be more profitable and proper than the situation as it exists.

Professional pride, Nader felt, would prevent most doctors and dentists from investing in the necessary improvements. He said they would look remiss if, after all these years, they suddenly decided to tighten up on X-ray safety. Nader said the proposed modifications would cost less than a day's revenue. But as he acidly remarked to interviewer Eric Norden of *Playboy:* ". . . but, of course, everyone knows that doctors and dentists, next to Negroes, American Indians and a few pockets of Appalachian miners, are the most impoverished economic groups in America."

Another Nader bête noir was the color television set. Unless its high voltage tubes are properly shielded, excess radiation is emitted. The recommended posture is to sit some six feet from your $700 monstrosity. Children sitting close to the set for many hours a day do face radiation danger if the set has not been properly shielded.

Nader says that the modification would have cost a dollar per set but the manufacturers weren't interested until one U.S. Public Health Service and a newspaper disclosed that some 100,000 sets of a major manufacturer were irradiating at levels of 100 to 1,000 times that set by the National Council on Radiation Protection and Measurements.

But radiation is not the only dangerous aspect of color TV sets. In 1969, some 10,000 sets caught fire; most of these—by a forty to one score—were color sets. The

National Commission on Product Safety has documented numerous cases where the sets caused complete destruction of property and loss of life. Poor insulation and sloppy product design were some of the factors cited by the Commission.

When the list of incidences were issued and identified by model and manufacturer, an industry spokesman complained that the incidences were actually "infinitesimal," to which Mrs. Harry Wheeler of Oak Lawn, Illinois who lost her parents in a fire started by a color TV replied: "Mr. [X] thinks [the fire hazard] is 'infinitesimal and not a great problem . . .' We lost our parents and [that] is not 'infinitesimal.' "

In its monumental and damning investigation of the ICC called *The Interstate Commerce Omission* written by senior Nader's Raider Robert Fellmeth, the Task Force found that abuses in the home moving industry were rampant and the primary target was the unprotected and defenseless consumer.

The Nader group reports that in 1968, some 600 million dollars was taken in by 183 inter-city movers. Some forty million Americans move each year, nearly twenty percent of the country's population. Every year the ICC receives some 5,000 consumer complaints, a large number considering the relative insularity of the regulatory agency. Congressmen and Senators receive many more from angered constituents who have had goods lost or damaged in transit, not delivered on time, or have had bills much higher than the original estimates quoted to them. As the Nader report succinctly capsuled the problem: "Perhaps the most important disadvantage of the small shipper is that he lacks legal *bargaining* power, the power to enforce his rights either in the courts or through the ICC."

Low estimates are usually the first headache. When the mover arrives with furniture and the estimate is fifty percent over what was originally contemplated, it's a bit of a shock. But what choice does the poor consumer have? He must pay by certified check, so he can't stop the check later. If he doesn't pay on the spot—no furniture. And the storage charges begin to accumulate until a decision is reached. Meanwhile, no furniture.

Most moves are booked through local booking agents who are paid on a commission basis. Thus, it is in their best interests to book as many moves as possible. A very easy and obvious way to keep business booming is to consistently underestimate.

The ICC and the home moving industry have tackled the estimate problem for over a decade. One solution voiced is that the estimates be made binding. The industry claimed that people would only show a part of what they intended to move, thus penalizing the mover. Adhering to estimates, also, according to the industry, would encourage underbidding, driving marginal movers out of the business. Such a situation would, of course, help the consumer, but would not please the industry. A third proposal called for deferring payment of the excess for 10 days, but the industry successfully beat this proposed regulation down, claiming much of the excess would be uncollectable. The ICC sided with the mover and the recommendation was killed.

Nevertheless, the low estimate persists. The Nader group came up with some interesting statistics right out of the ICC's own files. Out of 830,000 moves recorded by the ICC in 1960, there were some 72,000 underestimates of twenty percent or more. With increased labor and operating expenses in the intervening decade one can only surmise that the situation has deteriorated.

Early and late deliveries are another oft-repeated horror story. Sometimes, a family's possessions are transferred from van to van resulting in interminable delay. The ICC, however, does not require that the mover advise the consumer of this procedure until the van is ready to drive away. The mover must tell the consumer the route "when it is known," so it is advantageous for the mover not to say anything, even if he knows, because the law absolves him of responsibility on this score by a simple cop-out.

Most of the pick-up delays can be traced to overzealous local booking agents eager for business. On a smaller scale, there is a bump system whereby national companies who do a lot of business can get preference for their peripatetic executives and their families. In 1960 an ICC study found deliveries late thirty percent of the time with the period of delay ranging from a day to over a month. Early deliveries are another problem. One consumer who moved across country had his goods arrive ten days before the scheduled one and was socked with a storage charge which he had to pay to get his furniture delivered.

Tariffs are all but intelligible to the average consumer. Records are kept in Washington, but the consumer who is handed a bill and told to pay it or watch his furniture be hauled into storage finds this small consolation. The Nader Task Force quoted a source close to the industry who admitted that nearly half of those who moved in 1969 were overcharged. How the tariffs are established is another interesting fact. As the Nader report pointed out: "The movers are permitted, under special provisions of the Interstate Commerce Act which exempts them from anti-trust regulations, to engage in price-fixing by belonging to 'rate bureaus.' When the tariffs are increased, data to show that the increase is needed is supposed to be submitted, but their increases are rubber-stamped with the proviso that the movers show documentation next time."

The fact that the ICC has not put pressure on the moving industry to extend credit to the consumer, is just one more area of public arrogance on the part of the bureau. Any disputed amounts must be paid by the consumer, and then he must intitiate action to get the difference back.

On damage claims, the ICC found that fully a fourth of all moves had some complaint by the consumer. What's more, the movers never even acknowledge twenty percent of these claims. Why should they? They have their money. Let the consumer fume and sweat.

Besides the faults the Nader group found in the ICC's tender handling of the moving industry, it had some specific suggestions. Among them were: remove anti-trust immunity so that the consumer could benefit from competitive rates; make it possible for minority carriers to get started; provide consumer counsel for all home moving matters that come before the ICC; provide administrative action for quick dispatch of claims; simplify both bill of lading and tariffs so that they are really intelligible to the consumer; eliminate early and late deliveries by fining those companies; provide standards for packing, drivers and helpers, and complaint procedures.

The Nader group concluded: "The movers have so far been the beneficiaries of 'regulation.' They are protected from new competitors and from prosecution for collaborative price-fixing. While sheltered from competition on one hand, they have, on the other, been free from regulatory pressure to modernize, innovate, or even to provide adequate service."

Nader & The Quality Of Life

If Nader's concern with consumerism were to be put into one phrase, that phrase would be "quality of life." Almost everything he has done or written has been aimed at the protection, preservation and enhancement of human life. Obviously so in his fight for auto safety, against MSG in baby food, cyclamates, the not-so-hot hot dogs, unclean fish, all his chemical crusades; and not so obviously in his crusades for privacy, the investigation of Congress, and related subjects. He is not—as so many of his critics have charged—anti-business and free enterprise. He is pro-individual—determined to do what he can to improve each individual's quality of life, and try to get each individual aware enough to help himself.

And what could be more important to the quality of life on earth than the air we breathe? Also what could have more need of a joint effort than the clean-air projects?

Nader is especially concerned with our—and the rest

of the world's—problem with the poisoning of the air. Nader, of course, was not the first to be concerned, nor will he be the last, but Nader has a tendency to be stubborn, and once interested in a problem has a bulldog approach. He will hold on in spite of all difficulties and eventually—hopefully—our air pollution problems will be alleviated. Not by Ralph Nader, or by Ralph Nader associates alone, but by all of us.

The first truly comprehensive law on pollution was introduced by Senator Edmund Muskie and enacted in 1967. Like its predecessors, the Muskie-introduced bill provided for research, national standards for pollution emissions, Federal abatement, technical assistance, and Federal grants to the states. However, the Air Quality Act of 1967 also had its weaknesses.

The outline of the Clean Air Act of 1967 is basically as follows:

Step one—NAPCA designates "air quality regions"—an urban area and its environs that has common characteristics and patterns. It will be under its own individual standards, which still need to be set up by each state and local government involved. Enforcement also is up to the local government.

Step two—"Air quality criteria" and "control techniques" reports issued NAPCA described the effects of pollutants on human health and provides guidelines for action. The reports require the Federal Government to prove that each pollutant causes a specific effect before the local governments have to control it, and even when proven there are no laws forcing that control; there are only *guidelines*.

Step three—Each state must adopt standards for the various regions (there are 247 of them). Then a public hearing will be held before action can take place.

Step four—Finally, a plan of action for enforcing the standards must be developed by the states.

It is a lengthy process, taking up to fifteen months, and as the Nader-inspired report *Vanishing Air,* by John C. Esposito, points out, "the absurdity of this approach is underscored by the fact that this tortuous procedure must be repeated for each pollutant."

The lengthy process was not the only criticism leveled at the 1967 Air Quality Act by *Vanishing Air*. In it, Muskie himself is taken to task. Muskie had failed the nation, it said, because his bill was not tough enough. It had not included such necessary points as national emissions standards, federal regional commissions, and subpoena powers to demand data concerning emission. Also, his bill, the report continued, did not explore the possible power of the Federal Government, the irresponsibility of industry, the inability of local controls and the extent of the crisis. His emphasis on the regional rather than a combined Federal approach was enough, according to the report, to "warrant stripping him of his title as 'Mr. Pollution Control.'"

The publicity accorded *Vanishing Air* and particularly the attack on Muskie was extensive, but it was the first publicity of one of the Nader-associated reports that was not all good. Muskie, by this time, had a loyal following just as Nader had, and Muskie's supporters weren't taking the attack lying down; a rebuttal was issued detailing the inaccuracies of the report. It was pointed out that the report did not mention that fact that in 1970 Muskie proposed legislation that would impose fines of $50,000 and jail terms of up to five years for violators of the standards.

But whether the report was entirely fair to Muskie or not, the fact remains that regional jurisdiction seems doomed to failure. Certain areas of the country—especially the South—were so anxious to catch up economically with the rest of the country that their lobby-ridden governments have been heavily influenced by industry. A new industry wishing to locate in an area which is very anxious for more jobs is very likely to dictate its own terms, especially as far as pollution controls are concerned. It is often difficult for government officials to see beyond those dollar signs the industry represents to the distant future where the job opportunities and the dollar signs will mean little to people who can't breathe.

In his foreword to *Vanishing Air,* Nader wrote that the National Air Pollution Control Administration (NAPCA), which is the authority for air pollution in the

Department of HEW, has been almost ignored or shunted aside as irrelevant. The loss of belief that the government is capable of getting anything done about the problem of air pollution reflects a larger absence of confidence in our government in general. This report "probes deeply not only the failure of legislators and administrators to develop and deploy the law against air polluters but also the tragic distortion of the law and legal processess into shields for polluters against citizen participation and the public's health.

"Air pollution," he added, "and its fallout on soil and water is a form of domestic chemical and biological warfare." It has taken on the proportions of a massive crime wave, yet is not included in crime statistics. Corporate attitudes, feeling that pollution is the smell of progress, do little or nothing, keeping the facts from the people and waiting for the ecology thing to blow over. But what is needed is "sustained public demand for a liberation of law and technology to cleanse the air by disarming the corporate power that turns nature against man."

The study was undertaken in the summer of 1968 by a group of law, science, engineering and medical students who went to Washington to study the NAPCA, analyzing the agency's performance in conjunction with political and economic institutions in order to fully understand the successes and failures of the agency.

In Chapter One, titled "The Emergency," the report charged that there was no plan for an air pollution emergency. Just as most people who smoke cigarettes do not really comprehend the daily damage they are doing to their lungs, the American people do not comprehend the insidious poisoning they are receiving daily from industrial pollution. In fact, the danger is so pervasive that the term "excess deaths" is now being used to signify the number of deaths over and above the number normally expected, deaths which are connected to air pollution. For example, it is estimated that between 1,100 and 2,200 excess deaths in New York City annually are due to the amount of sulfur dioxide in the air.

A Nobel prize-winning geneticist, Dr. Joshua Lederberg, suggested in the Washington *Post* that our air could not even meet the quality standards for food additives, making our air unfit to breathe. The Muskie Subcommittee investigating pollution discovered that "the dramatic increase . . . in mortality from lung cancer . . . is now approaching epidemic proportions."

Among the epidemic "viruses" attacking us daily are airborne particles with such scientific-sounding names as benzoapyrene and hydrocarbons, and with such common names as carbon monoxide. Hydrocarbons have been definitely proven to be carcinogenic (cancer-producing), and more than half of the hydrocarbons in the air come from cars.

Benzoapyrene, a substance that all living creatures in a city breathe in daily, is taking its toll daily on our lungs. These particulates are produced primarily from burning coal and oil, and it has been discovered that that they cling to the stomach, esophagus, prostate, and bladder. Cancer in all these organs is on the increase.

These are scare tactics—but they are true, and very little is being effectively done about these horrifying truths.

Other chapters in the report attack the auto industry, specifically the internal-combustion engine, and recommends its replacement with the steam engine, which the report says is feasible and safe. A Senate Commerce Committee report concurs, stating that "a steamer produces almost no pollution." And still other chapters attack the major manufacturing sources of air pollution, the energy establishment, and the NAPCA, whose chapter is titled "Promises Deferred." Among the criticisms leveled at NAPCA are some of Nader's most used phrases—"extremely vague in action," "agreements are unenforcable," and "deadlines are too far in the future."

Perhaps those same criticisms could be hurled at the latest effort by legislation to clean up our air. Under the 1970 Clean Air Act, the Environmental Protection Agency has directed the states to produce plans for achieving by 1975 an overall air quality standard for sulphur oxide concentrations.

William D. Ruckelshaus, administrator of the Environmental Protection Agency, in 1972 underwent a probing of his agency by the Senate Subcommittee on Air and Water Pollution. Mr. Ruckelshaus reacted angrily, saying that "we live in a society in which institutions of government are mistrusted." (Echoes of Nader.) Furthermore, he said, the three days of hearings by the subcommittee into the administration's implementation of the 1970 Clean Air Act had "added to this distrust."

But little was decided at the hearing, only that Senator Thomas F. Eagleton, Democrat of Missouri, who was subcommittee vice-chairman, was not satisfied with Mr. Ruckelshaus' account of the roles played by the environmental agency and White House aides in what has become known as "The Anaconda case."

The Anaconda case concerned the effort by the Anaconda Company to get the Montana Board of Health to substitute less strict Federal standards from Ruckelshaus' agency for the Montana Board of Health's standards. It was insinuated that Ruckelshaus or someone from the agency had bowed to the copper company's pressure, and also that the final guidelines prepared by Ruckelshaus' agency had weakened enforcement of the 1970 Clean Air Act. A charge which appears to be all too true, and the Clean Air Act was too weak to begin with.

There are various other political rumblings in the area of pollution control, including those of President Nixon's. In his third environmental message to Congress, the President said he would seek legislation to combat sulphur pollution at its source. His method would be a tax levied against the sulphur oxides emitted by the companies themselves. Critics immediately rushed to prevent the passage of the legislation. The bill would be "a license to pollute," they said. Companies would still pollute, and would just add the pollution taxes to the end product. The consumer would end up paying for the pollution, which would still be uncontrolled.

That wasn't the only criticism leveled at Nixon's bill. Using the tax code as an enforcement weapon—which Nixon's bill proposed—wasn't exactly according to the Constitution, said some critics. And it is believed that

Wilbur Mills, a very powerful member of the House, also wonders about that aspect of the bill. And without Wilbur Mills . . .

In the area of air pollution by vehicles, trucks are the major source of pollutants. However, in 1972, the Environmental Protection Administration announced that it would delay for one year the implementation of anti-pollution standards on heavy-duty vehicles. The administration was convinced, said Deputy Administrator Robert Fri, that the manufacturers did not have enough time to apply to the new standards.

New proposals were then set to be applied for the 1974 model year, standards which would essentially match those *already in effect* in California. He said the proposals were based on technical feasibility.

But trucks were not the only vehicles which asked for and probably will receive a stay of execution. In March, 1972, a government technical committee urged that serious consideration be given to easing laws on air pollution by automobiles. The laws were scheduled to take effect in 1976. But in a report prepared for the Office of Science and Technology, the technical committee argued that national air-quality standards could not be attained in many urban areas in the specified 1975–77 time period, even if the exhaust-emission controls were enforced as now written.

Both Muskie and Nader immediately opened fire. Muskie said the report went along with the attack on the legislation by the three big auto makers—GM, Ford and Chrysler. Ralph Nader called it a sell-out to the auto interests and a "mockery of scientific integrity and competence."

It was, however, praised by the President of Ford Motor Company: "The government report on the costly effects of Federal regulations on the pocketbook of U.S. auto buyers and users can be the best news the public has had in years."

Good news?

Following are two of the recommendations of the committee:

1. Relaxing the Clean Air Act provisions limiting to 0.4 grams per mile the emission of nitrogen oxide to be allowed from cars, starting with the 1976 models. The committee suggested the limit could be raised to between one and two grams, that this would greatly cut costs, and that there would not be so many places where the effect would be damaging.

2. A two-car strategy which would require automobiles to have a tougher standard concerning nitrogen-oxide pollutants in more vulnerable areas, and allow a lesser standard elsewhere.

(Perhaps the two-car strategy would work as well as the now demised two-China policy?)

It would almost seem that the committee thought the air over one city or state stopped at their boundary like so many rooms of air in the sky. A typical news bulletin, maybe—"The air door over L.A. will remain closed today to keep their pollution contained. . . ."

In *Vanishing Air* the Nader study group recommended a steam car to replace the internal-combustion engine, but in Palatine, Illinois, Robert S. McKee would like to see an electric car as the replacement. He has built one which is powered by six 12-volt batteries and has an eight-horsepower motor. The car has a top speed of about sixty mph and can travel 150 miles before the batteries need recharging. McKee sees his car as a pollution-free answer to the second car for "around town" or commuting. Batteries can be plugged in in the family garage and recharged overnight.

But would the battery water pollute the waterways? Possibly, and that is certainly in the realm of Nader's concern. Two books on the subject of clean water came out of the Center for the Study of Responsive Law. The first, released initially as a report was *The Water Lords*, a study of the environmental conditions in Savannah, Georgia. The real focus was to be the ruination of the

Savannah River, but it carried into such areas as country tax structures, air pollution, industrial marketing philosophy, as well as politics, because all of these aspects of Savannah seemed to intermingle, complicating the real issue of how to clean the filthy river.

The villains of today in the pollution of the river are, naturally enough, the industries who spill their wastes into the water. Nader, in his preface, wrote, "The facts in this report compel an ethical conclusion. These Savannah-based companies are outlaws."

In the later book, *Water Wasteland,* the study group reported on the fifteen-year, three and one-half billion-dollar Federal water pollution control program. Their conclusion: the program had been a miserable failure. In only a few isolated areas, the report said, has the level of pollution on the nation's waterways been reduced by any appreciable degree. The report was prepared by David Zwick, a Harvard Law School student. He was assisted by Marcy Benstock and John Esposito, who was the project's co-director.

The most important failure of the Federal program has been its inability to control industrial pollution, because the responsibility for enforcement is left up to the states, which have—with few exceptions—come under the domination of industry.

Even the drinking water treatments now in effect almost everywhere are inadequate—inadequate because it seems almost impossible to keep up with the more than 500 new chemicals unleashed on an unsuspecting public each year by industries.

In a syndicated column Nader wrote early in 1972, he said that "nearly half of the nation's population drinks water that does not meet the weak, incomplete Federal water standards."

What is needed, Nader says, is a much more rigorous prevention and detection system, and more research into the contamination of drinking water. "It is time to face the facts, no matter how unsettling they may be. . . .

Responding belatedly to obvious disasters is not the mark of a rational society fully equipped to prevent them."

By failing to place specific limits on waste discharge, the federal agency made the Water Quality Act of 1965 unenforcable. And if that isn't enough, the Federal Government itself is one of the nation's single largest polluters. Nixon's Executive Order to agencies in the government to control their pollution is hopelessly inadequate at best.

The recommendations of *Water Wasteland* are that Federal pollution control officials be deprived of the discretion they now have to enforce the law or not, as they choose, and that a greatly expanded citizen role be effected in the "cleaning up pollution" program.

The clean-water programs cannot be stated seriously enough. We need water as much as we need air. In fact, by 1980, Americans will use an estimated 560 billion gallons of water a day, more than twice what was used in 1960. Soon, at that rate, there will just not be enough clean water to go around. It's hard to believe when one can turn on a faucet and watch all the clear liquid pour out on demand. But how long will it be before all the lakes and rivers and reservoirs are like the Cuyahoga River in Cleveland—which is a fire hazard. In 1969 the oil in the river actually burst into flames.

Meanwhile, the list of similarly contaminated rivers grows—the Buffalo, Escambia, Passaic, Merrimack, Rouge, the Ohio and the Mississippi. Not all of them as oily as the Cuyahoga, but they are polluted by other chemicals and poisons.

It is necessary for more people to become actively involved in the anti-pollution campaign, as Nader well knows. He has urged college students to join what he calls the "most powerful lobby this country has ever seen." He told them to hire scientists, ecologists and other experts, to become an "action-arm." He feels that such groups when coupled with the eighteen-year-old vote would form a lobby no industrial group could contend with.

As a spin-off of the pollution question, an interesting controversy is still raging concerning phosphates in detergents. It reached a climax of sorts about the middle of 1971, after which phosphates seemed destined to disappear from the marketplace, but now it appears they might be making a comeback.

It started early in 1970, or at least that was when the outcry reached major proportions. The problem with phosphates was not that they caused harm in any way to humans. In fact, phosphates are found in many foods, including beer and soft drinks. But the fact that it *is* a food is the problem, for organisms in our streams and rivers, such as aquatic weed and algae, also eat it. Because phosphates are one of the three important nutrients which the algae need, the excess of phosphates causes the algae to proliferate. A chemical process, occurring when an abundance of algae dies, reduces a lake's oxygen supply, which in turn kills other plant and animal life, which in turn effectively "kills" the lake.

In order to combat this problem, phosphates were denounced by the U.S. Government, and were replaced in many markets by non-phosphate brands. But the affair was not over. In September, 1971, the Surgeon General cautioned that some phosphate-free detergents are hazardous to human health.

The poor housewife was caught in a bind. Should she feel guilty or fearful about doing her laundry? It is a major dilemma which is yet to be resolved. And an area that Nader or his associates might look into, just as they have looked into other areas of the public health.

In a task force report on nursing homes, *Nursing Homes For The Aged: The Agony Of One Million Americans,* Nader wrote that "there is a colossal amount of collective callousness that pervades the society from the organization to the individual level. The most intense focus of what has been wrought for old people is the nursing home."

In 1970, Nader approached six seniors and an instructor at Miss Porter's School in Farmington, Connecticut. He told them of the project and they agreed—"enthusiastically." The study began that spring, a study which ranged from working experience inside several of the homes to a study of documents and complaints, and interviewing officials. "They saw the heart-rending tragedies firsthand."

Some of the findings of the report: Nursing homes are often unsafe, the care is poor, medical procedures are slipshod, government regulation of nursing homes is inadequate—all this about an industry which cares for at least one million senior citizens. As a remedy to the situation, Nader recommends that nursing homes receive Federal funds and that stricter enforcement of existing standards be imposed. He also recommends that a more rigorous review of medical licensing procedures be employed.

The report then was published as a book, *Old Age: The Last Segregation,* by Claire Townsend, project director. The book was reviewed by Edward Edelson in *Book World,* September 26, 1971. He said that "Ralph Nader made a mistake when he assigned a group of students . . . to conduct a study of old age and nursing homes. . . . They have produced a sober, forthright report which describes the worst abuses in our treatment of the aged and recommends sensible reforms.

"But one expects more than that from Ralph Nader."

What more does one expect from Nader? Well, Edelson feels that Nader has not lived up to his reputation of being a radical, then later says that Nader was never a radical to begin with. In fact, he says, Nader is "the best friend big business has had since Franklin Roosevelt.

"Businessmen must be stupid people indeed if they

fight to produce unsafe cars, unnutritious food, and a depressing old age for many Americans."

Maybe, Mr. Edelson, but it seems that's what businessmen are fighting to do.

In another of the Nader study group reports, *The Worker: Portrait of Nine American Job Holders,* the blue-collar worker, in whose ranks are more than eighty million Americans, comes under close scrutiny. Why?

Because, as Nader points out in his afterword, "the quest for meaning in work—as distinguished from the quest—is one of history's least charged courses. Man's struggle to make a living has always overshadowed the interaction of humans with their work and what it does or means for them."

The effects of business and government forces on the American life on a day-to-day basis are coming to public attention with increasing frequency. And certainly Nader and his study groups have been a large influence in bringing these things to the public's attention. These outside influences affect not only job efficiencies and attitudes, but, as we have seen, the air we breathe, the food we eat, and in short, our very lives.

And probably no one feels or notices it more than the blue-collar workers. It is this group within our society that is in the street both in a figurative and often literal sense, therefore having firsthand experience with the pollution and other problems. They are collecting garbage, directing traffic, wiping tables and floors, tightening bolts and hammering nails—usually living in the heart of cities or small towns, working under conditions frequently boring and adverse. Just getting by.

A consumer movement could do well to heighten the consciousness of the very vital element in our society. And vital they are. Numerous crippling strikes by these workers have brought home this fact to all the country. It is through this new awareness that on-the-job citizenship will develop, bringing the workers to expect their employers to operate with more fair play and corporate responsibility, which in turn will raise the quality of their lives and heighten their pride about their role and about themselves. There can be a new evaluation then of the meaning of work.

In December, 1971, at a formal session on Workers and the Environment during the 138th annual meeting of the American Association for the Advancement of Science, Nader said that an American worker probably faces less danger on dark city street than he does on a job. The industrial hazards of chemicals, pollutants and unsafe conditions "are four times more dangerous than street crime.

There is a need for a clear declaration that this is one of the worst and most savage forms of domestic violence," Nader said. Industry, government and labor are all responsible for the hazards of working, he continued, and further charged that industry doctors "are serfs, pure and simple," who are more concerned with protecting the company for which they are working than the workers they treat.

Since Nader believes that fines will never force big business to improve working conditions, he suggested another plan. Top executives, he said, should be penalized when hazards are found in the factories by being forced to work in the plants themselves for a specific amount of time. He said the lack of concern for industrial safety indicated that the government doesn't "value human life equally," since one billion dollars a year is spent on fail-safe devices for moon shots, but only thirty cents is spent for each worker on occupational safety.

Another area where workers are being cheated is in the tax structure. "Factory and office workers would not be taxed twenty percent of their wages while countless men of great wealth are assessed four percent or less and many who have enormous incomes pay nothing," Nader said, if things were equal for all. "Small businessmen and homeowners would not be made to pay inequitably burdensome taxes because large corporate owners of land, real estate and minerals pay far less than their required fair share."

All this is part of the quest for meaning in work, for importance as a citizen, for first-class treatment. And if this quest for meaning in work and a new value of self, of not only the blue-collar workers but of everyone else, is realized, will it be usurped again by the government and industry?

In a report commissioned by the American Civil Liberties Union, as part of its 50th Anniversary program, Ralph Nader touched on the invasion of individual privacy. Nader is the logical one to have written the article because of his famous GM affair, and he tackled it with the usual Nader thoroughness.

As part of an adaptation of that report printed in *Saturday Review,* April 17, 1971, Nader also indicated what you can do to protect yourself, most of which is covered in the Fair Credit Reporting Act, which became effective in April, 1971. The Fair Credit Reporting act entitles you to protect yourself against unfair credit ratings, and to be informed when an investigation of you is being undertaken. But as Nader points out—only if you take action are you protected! If you wish to, you can check your credit file periodically, "so that you can correct errors before they are reported and you are turned down" for further credit.

Nader's scope is wide. He has touched on the quality of life of the American Indian, his study group has looked into the medical profession and he has offered comments on such things as President Nixon's wage-price freeze.

In commenting on Nixon's freeze, he said it was the "single most expansive growth of unchecked executive power that has ever occurred." Nader said the mechanics of the freeze "symptomize an acceptance by use of our corporate state—big business, big labor and big government running the country without constitutional safeguards."

Nader also spoke out on the inequalities of the property tax. A key problem, he said, is that the tax is levied by about 80,000 different "Balkanized" local taxing jurisdictions across the country.

"Balkanization results generally in weak administration and susceptibility to political pressure and influence, but more specifically, it subjects each local unit to the tax blackmail practiced openly by large commercial and industrial firms, which exact legal and illegal property tax concessions by threatening to move to another jurisdiction."

Nader feels this problem could be solved by making property taxes statewide, rather than local. And he also feels that this goes along with the recent court decisions that have held the financing of education through the use of local property taxes illegal—because it leaves the amount of moneys spent per child dependent upon the amount of wealth in the community.

Nader has interest, it seems, in almost every aspect of human activity. He was even cited, by Charles McCarry in *Citizen Nader*, as playing a critical role in slain United Mine Workers of America official Joseph A. Yablonski's candidacy for the presidency of his union. How much influence and how much interest Nader played in that run for office is a matter of dispute. Nader says all he had intended was that Yablonski get a solid launching. But Yablonski's press secretary said that Yablonski felt Nader offered more help than he delivered. In any case, Nader was interested in the betterment of the union and he felt Yablonski's candidacy would help. He was interested because he felt that every wrong should be at least acknowledged.

"If we do not speak up in the public interest now, if we allow the problems to multiply, life in America could be intolerable. Perhaps impossible."

Nader Versus Business & Industry

Ralph Nader has always been concerned with poor products and services. However, there is something that he finds even more reprehensible—fraud and deceit which is concealed from the consumer and from which he has no recourse other than a wholesale boycott of the product in question.

Nader has said that the phrases used to describe the economy are rather nebulous and have no real pragmatic meaning to the consumer. Talk about "income levels," "inflation," and "government spending" do not articulate the ways in which the economy affects the consumer. Many tax dollars end up in the hands of big business without any accounting to the public. Cost overruns on defense projects, oil depletion allowances and farm subsidies to rich farmers are examples. At the level closest to the consumer Nader has recognized a particular kind of corporate malfeasance which is manifested in the products—adulteration of foodstuffs, worthless over-the-counter patent remedies, and a slew of inexpensive appliances designed for replacement rather than repair (toasters, hair dryers, shavers, etc.). Up to now this has been the main target of the consumer movement—to strike back at what is in front of your nose. Nader agrees that the consumer movement on this level has raised consciousness and enlightened many people, but that this type of action "has yet to devise the economic and political machinery that will counter-balance or deplete the power of corporations to impose involuntary expenditures."

There are many sub-economies where this type of strategy is of no use. At the retail level the consumer must pay for pilferage, corporate sloppiness, and outrageous overhead, costs built into the products. So not only is the consumer forced to absorb these effects but also the effect of business and industry on his environment. According to a Nader article in *The New York Review Of Books*, Senator Philip Hart estimates that of 780 billion dollars spent by consumers in 1969, 200 billion dollars was actually spent on nothing. Monopolies were able to make forty-five billion dollars by virtue of their price-fixing; oil import quotas drove up prices of fuel oil and gasoline an extra six billion dollars.

Nader does not only analyze problems—he has acted and acted decisively. An overview of his work and reports will prove this thoroughly. The issues attacked cover almost every facet of our lives: monopolies, banks, land ownership, water pollution, air pollution, food processing, airlines, Greyhound buses, and pipeline safety.

The Center for the Study of Responsive Law released an 1156-page report in June 1971 on anti-trust. Ralph Nader in his introduction to *The Closed Enterprise System* called this study prepared by his Raiders "a study of corporate radicalism so deeply insinuated into the politico-economic fabric of the society that a veritable revolution against citizens has occurred." Production took a full year with the help of a team of eight lawyers, two law students, and two graduate student-economists. Over

500 interviews were conducted and a complete survey of all the anti-trust literature was made.

Anti-trust, compared to other consumer and political issues, does not have a romanticized or especially appealing character to it. Its effect is more basic than that—it means higher prices are paid for goods by those industries which no longer have to compete with each other. As mentioned before, estimates are that this costs consumers forty-five billion dollars annually; some think sixty billion dollars is not an unlikely figure.

The report, according to project director Mark J. Green, started with three biases. First, that consumer welfare should be emphasized over business interests. Second, it is the anti-competitive structure rather than business conduct which is paramount in anti-trust violations. Third, the task force was wary of excessive private or public economic power.

One of the more stunning aspects that the report documented was the influence of Congress on merger and anti-trust activity. Concluded the report: "Congress is propelled by pressure, not principle, and until enough people tell it that anti-trust is important, until a political coalition coalesces which actively lobbies for consumer-anti-trust, Congress will continue its energetic indifferences."

A study of 1,000 firms that the FTC wanted to initiate in 1963 was stripped of prospective funds. Citing the lack of corporate data, the FTC pointed out how far such a study would have gone towards developing the full scope of the problem. Congress, under heavy pressure from various lobbyists, made sure that the funds were unavailable. The report feels that certain Congressmen don't want to tamper with the business support which keeps them in office. Even liberal Congressmen are caught in the same trap: Senator Vance Hartke is for steel quotas; former Senator Eugene McCarthy lent his support to the oil and drug industries; Senator Edmund Muskie wanted shoe quotas; Senator Jacob Javits represents "the

Street," commonly known as Wall Street, interests. And conservative politicians have traditionally upheld business interests.

The big problem, as the Nader Group sees it, is not so much the merger and conglomerate side, for the Department of Justice seems to watch over this area quite carefully. Rather it is the already existing monopolies which result in restraint of trade. For instance, take General Motors. Nader says: "General Motors is considered by many leading anti-trust economists and lawyers to have been in continual violation of the Sherman Act for years. The crime, however, has been just too big to tackle in the opinion of those who decide such matters in the Federal Administration."

The Closed Enterprise System specifically suggests that if the public is to receive the full benefit of the free market, shared monopolies should be broken up. The report recommended that the total assets of companies be limited under law to two billion dollars and that companies that exceed that amount be prosecuted under existing laws. The Assistant Attorney General for Anti-trust should be allowed to prosecute cases independently of the Attorney General. If such a proviso had been in effect the IT&T-Hartford Insurance merger would never have taken place. The two companies would have had to think twice about the feasability of such an operation, were political influence not such an important part of justice. The merger of the Justice Department anti-trust facilities and the FTC into a single roof to monitor anti-trust activities was another suggestion. The report recommended that the budget be increased fivefold to 100 million dollars. An increase in fines would only be fitting, as well as four month jail sentences for corporate offenders of the criminal provisions of the anti-trust law.

The prosecution of anti-trust cases also came under the Raider's scrutiny. Douglas Turner, former head of the anti-trust decision for three years under Lyndon Johnson, is kidded by the group for prosecuting a case against bull semen marketers but ignoring those against the auto and oil industries. Former Attorney General Nicholas Katzenbach is accused of bowing to political pressure and not really surveying the anti-trust scene with a keen eye.

Richard McLaren, head of the anti-trust division under Nixon, was given good marks by the study group for going after conglomerate mergers but low grades for failing to do anything about already existing business concentrations. McLaren evidently received some static from then Deputy Attorney General Richard G. Kleindienst. Kleindienst supposedly tried to block two cases that McLaren wanted to follow through on. McLaren, holding his own, managed to keep two major drug companies from merging and IT&T from acquiring Canteen Corporations. However, on the very crucial case involving the use of fuel oil in industries, McLaren was overruled by Attorney General John Mitchell.

In 1965 Continental, the number nine oil company in the country, decided to merge with Consolidation, the largest coal producer covering eleven percent of the market. This was during the time that Turner was head of the division. Urged by his subordinates to challenge the merger on the grounds that its precedent would pave the way for further mergers, Turner demurred. The result? Today twenty-nine of the top fifty coal companies, a little less than a third of the market, are oil company subsidiaries. Concluded the Nader Report. ". . . the petroleum industry, under the guide (sic) of diversification, is systematically buying up its competition." To break up the domestic oil cartel, the report recommended the oil import quota be eliminated and the oil depletion allowance be scrapped, among other things.

The political problems that face such a solution are almost insurmountable. Among those in government in Nixon's administration from the oil states are the former Secretary of the Treasury John Connally from Texas, Speaker of the House Carl Albert from Oklahoma, the Majority Leader Hale Boggs from Louisiana, Chairman of the House Appropriations Committee George Mahon from Texas, and Chairman of the tax-writing Senate Finance Committee Russell Long of Louisiana. Oil industries provide jobs in all their states. Some, like Long, even have proprietary interests. Oil's influence is not felt just on the level of Congress; it can affect presidential campaigns as well. During the 1968 campaign, Hubert Humphrey was promised heavy contributions by the Houston Petroleum Club if he promised to oppose any cuts in the oil depletion allowance. Humphrey refused. Richard Nixon seized the day and promised to maintain it. According to the Nader report, that was worth at least some $339,000 from three contributors. The report refers to an old Franklin Roosevelt quote: "The trouble with this country is that you can't win an election without the oil block and you can't govern with it."

Generally speaking the report was favorably received. Copious research and infinite detail would win the praise of legal scholars and economists alike. But an essay in the *New Republic,* a major Nader forum, was less than favorable. Richard A. Posner, a law professor at the University of Chicago who is considered to be an antitrust expert, lit into the report on several fronts. Said Posner: "It is a highly tendentious work, in which patent self-contradiction is never permitted to blunt a good sally." He further added, "The authors are not sensitive to inconsistency, nor are they curious about facts which do not square with their preconceptions . . . the authors have uncovered some genuine scandals; and my impression from my own experience in the Justice Department and my personal acquaintance with a number of the principals in the Study Group's account is that their reportage is highly accurate in the main . . . the Nader Study Group makes things seem both worse than they are and more readily remediable than they are, and this seems to me a dangerous combination of errors."

On January 4, 1972 Ralph Nader testified in a civil suit to upset the merger between International Telephone and Telegraph Corporation and Hartford Fire Insurance. Nader contended that William Cotter, who had been Connecticut State Insurance Commissioner when the deal went through and who had to approve the merger, told him that political and economic pressures had been exerted by IT&T. Cotter, who subsequently was elected to Congress in 1970, remembered differently. According to him, pressure came from individual IT&T and Hartford Fire stockholders. Cotter approved the merger, the largest in American business industry, on May 23, 1970.

Nader and Cotter met while addressing a meeting of insurance salesmen in March, 1970 in Hartford. In his testimony Nader said, "I expressed my concern about the legality of the merger and he expressed a similar concern. He was very upset that the hearings did not have interests testifying other than IT&T and Hartford Fire Insurance." IT&T, it seems, had rolled out the big guns to influence Cotter, subliminally or otherwise. Arriving in Hartford were a number of top IT&T executives including President Harold S. Geneen, one of the highest paid corporate heads in America with an estimated salary of $800,000 annually. Hartford Democratic leaders met with top IT&T people. The discussion of an IT&T-Sheraton Hotel for Hartford was supposedly on the agenda as was a possible contribution for the Hartford Civic Center, then under construction. Ironic that they should appear at the same time the case was being brought to trial concerning the merger.

Whatever the exact sequence of events was, Nader's suit was dismissed in Superior Court on March 29, 1972. Nader had claimed to appeal on the basis of special interest in consumer affairs. Judge Walter J. Sidor said that as Nader was neither affected in his property or other legal rights, the Nader suit had no standing. Apparently neither did any of Nader's co-plaintiffs, an IT&T shareholder, a Hartford Fire Insurance shareholder, and a policy holder with the insurance company. Nader's comment was that the merger had not been executed according to Connecticut law—the exchange of shares was not properly explained to the shareholders nor the nature of the anti-trust suit which had been lodged by the Department of Justice.

Another suit directly related to governmental influence á la Dita Beard/IT&T cause celebre was fought by Nader and his Public Citizen Inc. group in conjunction with the Federation of Homemakers and the Consumers Association of the District of Columbia. The suit on January 24, 1972 charged former Agriculture Secretary Clifford Hardin with reversing himself on a milk price stand in 1970 after more than $300,000 had been contributed to Republican campaign chests. Named as defendants in the suit were Earl Butz, the sitting Agricultural Secretary, and Commodity Credit Corporation, a purchasing arm of the Department of Agriculture. The suit called the decision illegal because it was based on political rather than economic considerations, stating that $322,500 were made through the political arms of three milk cooperatives. On March 11, 1971, Clifford Hardin had ruled there would be no increase in milk price supports. However, the Nader suit alleges that after a March 23 meeting between Hardin, sixteen milk interests, Nixon and White House operatives, Hardin reversed himself on March 25 and the milk supports were moved from $4.66 to $4.93 per hundred pounds. Nader says the net result is that retail prices of milk products were increased five percent and the increase cost consumers 125 million dollars in extra milk price support payments. Nader sought a rollback of the price supports to what he said was pre-fix level.

A week later the Justice Department filed an anti-trust suit against Associated Milk Producers, Inc, of San Antonio, Texas, the main producer named in the Nader suit of January 24. Associated was charged under the Sherman Act with illegal manipulation of Federal milk marketing orders, forcing those who hauled milk for co-op members not to haul it for non-members, as well as getting milk processors to agree they would not accept milk from non-members. These alleged violations are not the thrust of the Nader suit, but it is interesting to note that both suits came at the same time.

After the Department of Justice filed anti-trust suits against the three major television networks in April of 1972, Beverly C. Moore, associate director of the Nader Task Force which produced *The Closed Enterprise System* and a charter member of CARG, Nader's anti-trust monitoring unit, was moved to remark: "I didn't ever imagine they'd have the guts to do it."

He further told *New York Times* reporter Robert M. Smith: "The most important cases in anti-trust deal, like this one, with the structure of American industry, as contrasted with a little price-fixing here and a little price-fixing there. The Anti-trust Division has not pioneered in bringing these big structural cases."

In the summer of 1970 a lawyer and nine students went to Savannah, Georgia to study the environmental conditions under the direction of the Center for the Study of Responsive Law. Led by Project Director James Fallows, the object of the excursion was to show how intertwined are corporatism, ecology, taxation and government and how strong is the influence of the first on the others. "The facts in this report compel an ethical conclusion," said Nader in his introduction to the report. "These Savannah-based companies are outlaws." The report, *The Water Lords,* was published in 1971.

The focus of the project was, of course, the ruination of the Savannah River. No one thought the investigations would cover areas such as industrial marketing philosophy, county tax structures, air pollution of course, and politics. But it was the same political and economical issues that created the filth in the river, the dirt in the air, and prevented proper ecological action that involved all these issues. James Fallows says the public thought Nader's Raiders used special, secret tactics for gaining information, but no special abilities or secret contacts were employed. Rather, all that was needed was time and effort for gathering facts and interviewing people.

Savannah's life has traditionally centered on the river, with the port the core of the town's economic life. A seemingly unlimited supply of water (due to the fact that it receives forty-six inches of annual rainfall) led to an assumption that the people could do almost anything they wished to the river, including use it for a sewer. Warnings about the conditions of the river were unheeded; a newspaper analysis in 1879 did little to alter habits. The people could still fish successfully and stroll peacefully along the clear riverbanks, so they did not react to criticism.

The big change came in 1935 when the Union Bag Company, now Union Camp Corporation, brought a factory to town. They, too, used the Savannah River as a sewer. Civic committees' anxieties in 1936 were ignored and today the uses and beauty of the river have been reduced to one: a garbage disposal. Even without statistics and facts, the damage is obvious—long, brown wedges can be seen trailing from company areas in the water: lines of foam run along the banks and spread out over the entire river; there is the odor of human excrement: sometimes the water in front of City Hall actually boils as hydrogen sulfide and methane gas rist from the sludge at the bottom of the riverbed; dead fish can sometimes be seen floating along; in places the water has seared the skin off small children.

In 1965 engineers estimated a city sewage treatment plant to cost 10.8 million dollars and to be completed by 1968; five years later, the estimate had swollen to twenty-one million dollars and would hopefully but not positively be finished in 1973. This five-year, ten-million dollar difference can be attributed to politics. Mayor Malcolm MacLean, sensitive to his constituents' needs and desires, chose not to issue a tax until after he was voted back into office. However, he continued to make sure that plans went smoothly and slow progress was being made on the construction. The voters, however, chose instead to elect J. Curtis Lewis, a conservative, to office. Lewis and his aldermen found themselves in the middle of a bizarre chapter of the sewage story—the Sewell-Wiedeman feud. A local engineer, Dan Sewell, had longed for the building contract to design the city sewage treatment plant. Upon discovering he had not received it, he launched a campaign against the selected engineer, Theodore Wiedeman, accusing him of assorted violations of professional ethics. Lewis, left with a program that was expensive, with no apparent virtues for the immediate time, and designed by a man supposedly incompetent, chose to wait until the verdict was handed down. Wiedeman's license was revoked in September, 1967. Lewis then asked R.S. "Rock" Howard, head of the Georgia Water Quality Control Board to review Wiedeman's plans and offer advice. His office gave it full approval. In March, 1968 a Superior Court judge restored Wiedeman's license, claiming he had been the victim of a kangaroo court. These two events did not help to bring action on the project, however. Howard felt it necessary to threaten legal action at this point. Lewis reacted by requesting another review of the plan, postponing building once again, until the selected review firm, Engineering Science, approved the plan in November, 1968. Throughout the next year, monies could be found to finance a thirty-million dollar expressway, a bridge to a local landmark island, and restoration of historical homes, but the city was stalling when it came to the amount needed for the treatment plant. Lewis and his men finally decided that the city's proper share of expenses was twenty percent according to Public Law 660, which provides that the Federal Government will finance fifty-five percent of the cost if the state will finance twenty-five percent.

Despite lobbying, the state government has yet to endorse its share of the expenses. Meanwhile construction has begun and it appears that it will be the newly-elected mayor's responsibility to iron out the problems.

American Cyanamid produces titanium dioxide, a white pigment used to write the m's on M&M candy, among other uses. Some six million gallons of waste water containing sulfuric acid are released daily in its manufacture. Most forms of aquatic life are so sensitive to the acid-alkaline balance that even small changes can result in cuts in respiration rates and death of fish. The large amounts of iron which flow from the companies' pipes create such a huge COD (Chemical Oxygen Demand) that 25,000 to 35,000 pounds of dissolved oxygen are withdrawn from the river. Aside from this daily assault, Cyanamid was responsible for one of the worst disasters to the river. Because they are only permitted to release acid on the outgoing tide, the company uses large holding ponds to store its wastes. Built on land known to be marshy and unstable, a torrential rainfall on July 17, 1968 caused a fifty-foot section of the dike to cave in and release thirty million gallons of water containing 3.½ million pounds of raw sulfuric acid into the river. The amount of fish that died covered miles and miles of river area; the long-term effects of the spawning grounds were unestimable. Cyanamid's solution was to build a larger, broader dike—not a guarantee that this won't also give way to the next heavy rains.

Union Camp of Savannah has the biggest kraft paper plant in the world, yet has made only the most reluctant progress in cleaning up the river, consistently violating even the low standards set by the state water control agency. In defense of the company's policies at an enforcement conference in 1965, the representatives even went so far as to say that perhaps the mill pollutants were not really dangerous: "They do not constitute a health hazard. In proper quantities they contribute food to the small organisms which provide food for fish." The result of the conference was that each river plant would have to cut its BOD (Biological Oxygen Demand) amount by one-fourth and reduce the amount of settleable solids by ninety percent by the end of 1967.

Test after test proved that Union Camp was consistently violating the pact even into 1970. Its average BOD exceeded that allowed by the water control board. However, even this is not indicative of the true damage for it is only an average, and it is on days when pollution output is high that most damage is done. Union Camp lacks a back-up system, so that when something goes awry in the cleaning system, unpurified water is sometimes released into the river. Claims of spending ten million dollars in ten years sounds pathetic when it is known that this is merely one-third of one percent of the company's revenue over the same period. An example of Union Camp's concern for the river, its respect for law and its honesty is exemplified by the following incident: The U.S. Coast Guard discovered an oil spill emanating from Union Camp's factories which violated the Refuse Act of 1899 (still the strongest law on the books). Pleading *nolo contendere,* the company was convicted, given a suspended sentence and placed on a year's probation. Two weeks later, the Coast Guard found the second oil spill. Three times throughout the summer the Task Force asked a company representative about the spills, but he denied that a second spill had taken place. Upon being shown the Coast Guard report, however, he began to remember some details of the incident, trying to make a distinction between the type of oil which was spilled and what the report said, then launching into an attack on the Coast Guard for violating private property rights.

In 1966 a ship crashed into the leg of a bridge due to heavy "fog"; early in 1970 drivers panicked in a cloud of smoke and one lady crashed; local pilots have to use radar to land on Travis Field. All this danger due to the density of the air would be enough to endure, but

Savannahians have the added attraction of suffering the distinctive stench of the paper mill odor.

The mills cling to a nineteenth century philosophy that the public does not need to know what is being emitted from their smokestacks. Under the new Air Quality Act of Georgia, companies were required to fill out forms answering air environmental questions. Union Camp did not even submit a completed form. While American Cyanamid did complete the form, they did so at about the same time that they were finishing up a new processing system that would permit some emission of the deadly chlorine gas into the atmosphere.

There are available technological processes that could clear the air, but the enforcement laws here aren't strong and nothing appears to be undergoing any great restraint.

Every decision that the town of Savannah makes about its mill is prefaced by a theory which, briefly stated, is: "The town was on the verge of collapse until the arrival of Union Camp. The company, by providing 5,000 steady incomes, saved the town, a fact which leaves its eternal gratitude to the company. The townspeople were in such a state of panic over their situation in the 1930's that they thought industry was the only answer, and it led them to bargain away many of the town's most valuable assets. Union Camp ended up with a prime plant site at almost no cost, low-cost financing for four million dollars, a guarantee of no local competition and protection from complaints about its pollution. All this to a company that had been floundering financially up north. Many Savannahians feel a vague threat that the company will leave if threatened or pressured too much, but it is highly unlikely that Union Camp could find another site with such geographical virtues and tolerance. Besides, the cost of moving is almost a preventive measure in itself from this venture.

Besides jobs, the mills like to think they have brought opportunity to the South. Unfortunately, the South still has some of the worst cases of poverty in the country—

the region surrounding Savannah is considered to be one of these depressed areas. The mills also seriously cut the city's chances for attracting new industry, for the natural resources are being utilized by the occupants already there. They are also ruining the town's tourism, a trade which the Georgia Institute of Technology estimated in 1965 to be the town's biggest prospective industry. Raw sewage and stinking vapors from the river, clouded over by a continuous offensive-smelling haze are dimming future tourist trade prospects, however.

"With the possible exception of its air pollution, there is no way in which an industry can more directly harm its townspeople than through manipulation of the local tax system . . . In Chatham County and Savannah over the last decade, taxes have risen so sharply that they are considered the major local problem . . . By most calculations, the largest landowner, Union Camp, shortchanges Chatham County by three to four million dollars every year." The formation of tax zones provides a permanent shelter within the industrial zones. The industries could never be annexed to the city and therefore never have to pay city taxes. Most cities do provide easy or no taxation to new industry; Savannah is the only one that continues to practice this indefinitely. Attempts on the part of city councilmen to change the circumstances have resulted in indignant outcries from the industries, who paint dark pictures of doom—could they be veiled threats—and demand that the city remain honorable and live up to its end of the bargain.

Another aspect of the problem is conflict of interests. Ever since Union Camp's initial arrival, the Citizens Bank and the company have been inseparable business allies. In 1970, the chairman of the Chatham County Commission was vice president of the bank; another commissioner is a nephew of the bank's president; another old business partner of a large real estate and construction company. The Commissioner in charge of Finance is an executive of Union Camp. While other companies are willing to admit that it is almost impossible to separate interests and therefore discourage the holding of political offices among its employees, Union Camp actually "encourages its employees to take an active part in their community."

Nader selected Savannah almost arbitrarily, but with enough time and resources it could have been any American city. The conclusion was that "if the industries stop polluting the Savannah River, they will be able to use ground water. At the same time, fishing and its revenue would increase. If Union Camp and the other industries nestled in their tax shelters paid their fair share of taxes, Savannah would easily have been able to afford its sewer system long ago. If the air were free of kraft odors and the river free of raw sewage, Savannah's efforts to attract tourism and other industries would pay off."

The Task Force offered a number of suggestions for getting action on environmental issues:

1) Strengthen the Georgia air and water quality laws.
2) Monitor ground water usage.
3) Speed up construction of sewage treatment plants throughout Chatham County.
4) Reform the tax system.
5) Require quarterly progress reports from Savannah's polluters.
6) Hold another abatement conference.
7) Promote citizen commitment to environmental issues.

A broader study of water problems was compiled by another Nader Study Group. Their report was released as *Water Wasteland* in April, 1971. It was the product of twenty-one months of research and resulted in the 700-page study. David Zwick, a Harvard Law School student and co-director of the project, prepared the report.

More than fifty percent of all waste comes from industry, the study found. Many states, however, desperate for industry, do not enforce pollution statutes in order to avoid offending the makers of the jobs they need so desperately. Despite a public relations blizzard, the report found corporate polluters are spending little on pollution control. The most progressive companies are putting about seven-tenths of one percent of their revenues into this area. The average figure is closer to two-tenths of one percent. Federal and state enforcement of a variety of pollution statutes was found to be distressingly low.

"Because banks and their regulatory agencies treasure secrecy to an extreme, what goes on behind the marble pillars is, to the public, off limits," said Ralph Nader in his introduction to *Citibank,* a 547-page preliminary report on the First National City Bank of New York. A sixteen-member Task Force researched the information, released in June, 1971. "It is the belief that information flows about banks to the public should be greatly increased . . . that prompted this study." The idea was to see what banks were and were not doing for the consumer. *Citibank* was focused on First National City because of its agressive leadership and huge size.

The bank was not overly pleased to be the focus of such an inquiry, warily extending cooperation to the Nader group, but remaining true to its advertising jingle, "First National City hates to say no."

The report does not pretend to cover all aspects of the bank's operations. For instance, the bank's trust activities and its overseas operations were not touched in this first draft. The main focus of the preliminary report was to examine the bank's conduct along the "community-consumer-employee-city-regulatory agency" axis. Relations between bank and customer were also discussed although not to as exhaustive and conclusive an extent as could be. Various areas of consumer banking such as in-bank service, Master Charge, collection practices, and mortgage arrangements were covered. It explored First

National City Bank's (FNBC) corporate banking policies including lending, deposits, the granting of credit, mergers and acquisitions, minority business, and the bank's Board of Directors. Its role within New York City was looked at: the city's checking account, state and municipal bonds, short term debts, disposal of the Long Island Railroad, erection of the World Trade Center, and the touchy matter of bank taxes. The final discursive part of the study examined bank regulation by the Comptroller of the Currency and the Federal Reserve Board and Congress. A seven-page list of recommendations concluded the report. David Leinsdorf headed the Task Force of sixteen members, working out of the Center for the Study of Responsive Law, Nader's home base. Together they conducted over 400 interviews with bank officials, bank customers, government money managers, staff personnel of various regulatory agencies, and Congressional committee staff members. Questionnaires were sent to individuals and corporate bank members alike.

As mentioned previously, the bank extended marginal cooperation to the Task Force. Out of 37,000 employees only fifty-three were allowed to be interviewed, a mere handful for each Task Force member. The bank was quite careful about how the interviews were to be conducted, for at each one representatives of the bank's senior management as well as the Vice-President of Public Relations attended. Also present was a member of the bank's legal staff. Interviews were tape-recorded and did not take place in the individuals' offices.

FNCB refused to provide the Task Force with any information about a specific customer relationship, the names of corporate securities for which FNCB is trustee, or a list of the bank's lawyers. Leinsdorf, in attempting to ascertain who some of the major stockholders were, was shown several large-bound volumes but not allowed to take notes; he could only look. However, he sent a registered letter to another member of the bank's hierarchy asking why no copying was permitted. On a subsequent visit he was allowed to gather the material he needed. Other top-secret information included: loans to directors affiliated with subsidiaries; the size of its loans to such "troubled borrowers" as Lockheed and Chrysler Corporation; the volume of Master Charge credit; a geographic breakdown of its mortgage portfolio; the average salary paid to employees in a particular job classification; the profitability of the bank's various divisions; and the bank's role in financing mergers in the oil industry.

FNCB is the largest bank in New York with 200 branches, twenty-five percent more than its nearest competitor. It is second only to California's Bank of America for winning the heavyweight title of the country. FNCB has contact with more consumers, however, for it has more individual deposits and extends more individual credit than any other. It was the first in many consumer-oriented areas as well: to make money available to consumers; to enter into the lucrative foreign market (it has 630 branches in eighty-two countries now); to devise a negotiable certificate of deposit providing corporate investors with a viable alternative to Treasury Bills as a short-term investment; and to develop a one-bank holding company. All these services have certainly paid off. Citibank's deposits have doubled in the last seven years, its loans and assets have grown 100 percent in six years, and its profits and number of employees tripled in a decade. Its assets are twenty-six billion dollars; only four other American Corporations have the same or more assets. These are AT&T at fifty billion dollars, Prudential Life Insurance at twenty-nine billion dollars, Metropolitan Life Insurance at twenty-eight billion dollars, and the Bank of America at twenty-eight billion dollars. Besides its own hoard of assets, FNCB manages some twelve billion dollars in pension funds, private trusts, and other investment accounts.

Despite all the "advances" FNCB has made, a management consulting firm conducted a study in 1970 which showed that the quality of customer service has sharply decreased over the past decade. The Nader Report's assessment of that study read in part: "Bankers now keep customers waiting, even when the bank is not busy, fail to explain the cost and operation of the services and exhibit little courtesy, friendliness or efficiency in their dealings with customers."

A dim view was taken of what was called the bank's excessive default judgement rate by use of "sewer service," wherein the defendant in such action never receives notice until the default action has been entered. The report recommended that the U.S. Department of Justice bring suit against Citibank as well as have previous default orders vacated and the money returned to the debtors who were the victims of such action. The sewer service charge was leveled at not just FNCB but at the wide variety of banks and businesses that receive default judgements by such a method. The Task Force called for: ". . . a broad class action statute, giving citizens, whose individual claims are generally too insubstantial to justify the enormous cost of litigation against private corporations with their endless legal resources, the right to sue *en masse* to enforce the law. This would obviate the need to expand existing or create new government bureaucracies to enforce the law."

New York City is in the midst of a desperate housing crisis that can only grow worse. FNBC has about two billion dollars in personal savings deposits, yet only about one-fourth of this total has been allotted for mortgages. However, the Group reports that employees of certain corporate interests have been given mortgages while the general public searches in vain for sufficient funds to renovate existing property and is expected to perform the almost impossible task of trying to build new homes within the city limits. Citibank's moral commitment extends only to its favored customers and not to the city in which it does business, that same city that is falling down around many of the bank's branches.

Until high turnover forced it to re-evaluate its practices, FNCB made a high school diploma a requisite for even the simplest clerical jobs. But an annual turnover of more than 5,000 employees forced the bank to adopt less rigid criteria. However, the "opportunities for blacks, women, Jews, and other minorities to move into positions of responsibility are still very limited." The problem is a simple one—there are more candidates for promotion than there are promotable positions to be filled. The end result is employee dissatisfaction leading to poor consumer service either by omission or commission. According to the Nader survey, blacks make up about a third of all those employed by FNCB; only four percent of the "platform personnel" (employees behind desks rather than counters) are black. Of some 288 officers in the Corporate Banking Group, only one black could be found—an assistant cashier with no lending authority. Over half of the employees are women. Yet there were only three women in the Corporate Banking Group and just one single woman vice-president. The 1970 Management Consultant study found that many women who were on the platform performed better than their male counterparts. Despite these facts, few women have made it up into the inner sanctums of Citibank.

While the Nader report uncovered a lot FNBC was not doing, it also uncovered a lot about just what the bank was doing with its resources. The results of these efforts, if proven true over the long run, do not look good for the consumer.

The report revealed that in 1970, FNBC had interlocking directorates with forty of the country's top 300 largest corporations, including seven of the top ten. The report also showed that some of the largest corporations, who were in grave financial straits, were able to obtain credit at the prime rate—supposedly reserved only for those with spotless credit ratings. Citibank was instrumental in arranging marriages between corporations. Often local banks were drained when the parent company came in and had the assets transferred to Citibank. So, money made on a corporation based in Missouri might be siphoned off and put to work in New York, leaving the local bank short on money for mortgage and personal loans as well as larger sums necessary for commercial development.

New York City's relationship with FNCB is an unhappy one. The report claimed that: "Preferential bank income taxes cost New York City ten million dollars a year in lost revenues." The banks have gotten out of the municipal bond markets, adding millions of dollars to the city's borrowing costs. Its direct influence in the domestic affairs of the city has not gone unnoticed: "FNCB was represented on a commission appointed by Governor Rockefeller that recommended a sixty-five million dollar giveaway to purchase the long-bankrupt Long Island Railroad from a major FNCB debtor."

FNCB also processes New York City's personal income tax returns. Citibank retains copies of the data, despite the fact that its contracts prohibit the use of such data. But with the growth of the dossier and the data bank, it would be less than candid to think FNCB has kept all this information on file as a public service.

The Comptroller of the Currency and the Federal Reserve Board, both of whom keep an account at Citibank, have approved thus far of its most striking business triumphs, like the formation of a one-bank holding company, a corporate affiliation which permitted the bank to "engage in many activities prohibited to banks."

To summarize, the report's conclusion is that the FNCB smiles on business and frowns on the individual consumer—unless he's allied with business. The fundamental issue facing banks and their branches is whether they will be allowed to construct bigger business enterprises and extend even greater influence into the marketplace or whether consumers, aided by government, will come to the fore and say once again that banking is a public trust to be operated away from the field of partisan play.

The report devoted seven full pages to what FNCB might do to start getting back on the right track. Among the suggestions were:

1) Increase minority opportunity.
2) Clarify elliptical advertising and promotional material.
3) Abandon sewer service and higher-paid process servers.

4) Encourage minority business development.
5) Start putting money back into the city through mortgages.

Other specified recommendations were made to the bank as well as to the Comptroller of the Currency, New York City, New York state and municipal governments, the Federal Reserve Board, the U.S. Department of Justice, the Internal Revenue Service, and Congress.

The results of the study drew comments such as "amateurish" and "inaccurate" from those close to the bank. Senator Jacob Javits of New York, who the report had charged with receiving "political contributions in disguise," responded by stating that the accusations were "deplorable, reckless, careless and entirely untrue." The First National City Bank said the study was "based on serious misconceptions about the proper role of the banking system and a frightening cynicism about other people's ethics." Nevertheless, the bank said, "The report will be given careful consideration in our continuing reappraisal of Citibank's policies and practices."

The interlocking between government and business is a continuing subject of fascination to Nader's forces. *Power And Land In California,* a 900-plus-page report, was released by Nader in August 1971. The twenty-five-month investigation by a score of the Raiders was headed by Robert Fellmeth, co-author of the first Nader report on the Federal Trade Commission who was also the principal author of *The Interstate Commerce Omission.* With the release of *Power And Land* Fellmeth became the first Raider to score the literary hat-trick.

The study group found that twenty-five landowners hold more than thirteen percent of all the privately-held land in California. Another recent study showed that forty-five corporate farmers own sixty-one percent of six million acres of farmland surveyed by the study. The breakdowns inside individual counties are even more significant. The top twenty landowners generally held from one-third to one-half of the total land in the county. The size of the average farm has grown from 224 acres in 1930 to 627 acres in 1969, a problem further aggravated in that Federal and state governments generally let abuttors have first shot at adjoining public lands as they go up for grabs.

Some landowners were found to be holding their lands illegally. The task force cited Southern Pacific, the state's largest landowner, which should be forced to give up its massive holdings. They claim the company "continues to flagrantly violate the terms of land grants" and is "using them for income production contrary to land grant terms."

The report noted the emergence of an "army" of 235 lobbyists allied to the "land interest complex" at the state legislature in Sacramento. On the consumer or environment side there are three groups, none of which can touch the land interests in financial power. Much prime agriculture acreage is being lost as what the report characterizes as "unnecessary development" takes place in the state. Not all of this is the result of building directly on farm land; urban sprawl is a contributing factor, for as the cities head toward the country, farmland assessed valuation goes up as does its taxable value. The farmers can usually sell at a profit, so the developers have hop-scotched further and further over the land and the pattern of urban sprawl assumes a completely random character. The study contends that the state's Williamson Act, designed to prevent such sprawl, is a colossal failure. Low assessments are made of non-productive land, making it more profitable for speculators to just hold on to their land and wait.

Despite the state's avowed intention to help and encourage the family farmer, the benefactors are actually the corporate owners like Standard Oil of California. According to the report, the corporate farms ". . . get tax breaks, discriminatory credit terms, and take extreme advantage of their political power . . ." The net result of the rise of corporate involvement has been the rise of prices, decreased availability, and land rendered useless by poor usage. Price supports and other subsidies also help the large corporate farmer. As does the lack of pollution controls which allow him to trade long-term environmental status for short-term gain.

Power And Land In California recommends the following agricultural reforms: 1) Land speculators should be charged a high "zoning-up" fee before they subdivide; 2) a higher capital gains tax at a rate higher than taxation of regular income, designed to discourage wild speculation; 3) a state land survey to catalog the use of agricultural and other land; 4) the end of price supports and other subsidies to large corporate farms; and 5) elimination of conflicting interests from state agencies regulating agriculture.

Water is a vital necessity for agriculture. In California, mainly a dry state, the use and conduct of water is regulated closely by the state. Three-quarters of the water used is provided by irrigation. The Nader Group looked carefully at the California Water Project. The State Department of Water Resources that sponsored the project claimed that it was costing 2.8 billion dollars to run the project, but the group concluded this as a gross underestimate and that the actual cost was closer to nine billion dollars. According to the Department, ninety percent of the cost of the project would be borne by the project's customers. In fact, the study group found that figure closer to thirty-eight percent, leaving the taxpayers to pick up the fifty-two percent difference. There were then four groups of benefactors from the water project: land speculators whose land, receiving irrigation, would now become commercially feasible; the building trades involved in the construction of the project itself; a thousand corporate farmers in the San Joaquin Valley; and those businesses in Southern California which utilize a large amount of water—like Standard Oil, which purchases "excess" water from the Metropolitan Water District of Southern California. The Metropolitan Water District is committed to buying more water than it needs from the water project in order to well it at discount rates to its large-volume customers.

The group examined the state's highly-touted Porter-Cologne Water Quality Control Act of 1969 and found it to be wanting. They claimed to have "found a law written by polluters and for polluters, weakened further by nonenforcement." Polluters had a chance to soften the effect of the act at every step of the writing. Furthermore, "the law is administered by a system of legalized conflict-of-interest." Corporate and municipal polluters openly pollute without any fear of intervention. The stiff $6,000 a day penalty set for polluters has never been levied against any offenders (at least as of mid-1971).

The fourth part of the report examined California's wild areas where "forests are leveled, the desert is bulldozed, lots are staked out and sold purely as speculative investments . . ." These are erstwhile vacation developments where basic services such as water and utilities are practically non-existent. Few dream houses ever go up. In one county, Madera, over 21,000 lots had been cleared in twenty years but only 100 houses dot the land. Surrounding wildland is exposed to erosion, damage to its watershed, siltation, loss of its animal population, pollution and other forms of contamination. Other problems include protection to endangered species and thermal pollution. Parks and coast land now are dwindling as the need for recreational area increases. Recreational, industrial and commercial developers have had a field day lying to both prospective customers and the local governments that their subdivisions will presumably "benefit" the public. Witness Pacific Gas & Electric, however, who gave up a site for an atomic reactor, only when a fault was discovered under it.

Part Five of the report concerns new development. California's population boom in the last thirty years has generated an immense demand for shelter. Site has always been a primary consideration because of the earthquake threat. The demand has increased to such a point that now developers have been found to be building on land that is literally giving way under foot. Little has been done to help minimize the effect of these frequent earthquakes, by the way, although more advanced warning techniques and building techniques exist.

Unscrupulous speculators abound. One group of interests induced people to locate in an arid desert sixty miles from the nearest city. Industrial development was encouraged with no thought for city planning. And then a huge airport was added. On the date the airport was to be approved, the local contingent couldn't attend the opening, for the superhighways out to the site were washed out by floods. There is the case of one developer who had grossed over 102 million dollars from lot sales in thirteen years. The report contended that many of the representations made to lot buyers were fraudulent—a pasture was described as an "international airport," a deserted barracks as an industrial "park." Existing water, good weather, a school system and booming industry at various sites were all selling points that were discovered to be untrue. The state attorney general, aware of these goings-on, took no action, according to the report.

"The local property tax is a political tax," contend the Raiders. Inequities were documented where individual homeowners paid at a rate twice that of industry. In addition, government could work toward curbing inefficiency and irregularities, but it is not.

The state has an immense commitment to the automobile (with its hidden subsidies like air and water pollution) and highways. The placement of roads near developments is a windfall to landowning speculators. One town of 1,000 is currently having a road built which will make it accessible from five directions as well as destroy miles of parkland and endanger rare species of sheep. One local legislator, when asked by the Task Force about the new road, replied that the people wanted it. When told his files showed 867 negative comments to fourteen favorable, he replied, "To hell with the people."

The State Legislature as a vehicle for conservation forces is almost useless in California. 1970 was a year when "ecology" and "environment" were the hot words of some 300 bills that were introduced by pro-conservation forces. Yet only fourteen of these were considered vital and only two of the important bills were passed, in watered-down form, no less. The 235 land interest lobbyists spent about 3.6 million dollars in 1970—$30,000 a legislator. Campaign donations in large measure are also there for legislators who cooperate. Some sixty percent of the Assembly and fifty-five percent of the Senate had outside jobs connected with the land interests before they joined politics. Obviously laws against such employment practices within government are rarely enforced. Any clean-up of California must begin with the legislature, who must enact necessary laws in order to make a clean environment a reality.

Ralph Nader, in his introduction to *Power And Land In California* sums up the crisis in the Golden State: "The utter disregard for the integrity of the land and its relationship to man by powerful corporate executives, together with smaller participants caught up in this frantic cycle of devastation, inflicts special penalties on the young and unborn who are so little represented . . . the demands on our national resources are now much greater and much more critical. And time is not so plentiful for the exercise of indifference."

One line in Nader's stock speech goes like this: "GM would buy Delaware if DuPont would sell it to them." DuPont has been in Delaware for over 170 years and its influence permeates every aspect of the state's life. Some of them, as listed by the Nader Task Group, are: industry, commerce, finance, government politics, education, health, transportation, media, charitable institutions, environment, land, recreation, public works, community improvement groups, taxation, and even the air the people breathe (polluted). The DuPont payroll of 288 million dollars is bigger than Delaware's state budget. Thirteen percent of Delaware's work force are supported by it. Two of the state's largest banks are controlled by DuPont. The state's most influential newspapers are owned by the family. The only U.S. Representative from Delaware is Pierre S. DuPont IV; the governor, Russell Peterson, is a former employee of the company; in fact, by one count a quarter of the state legislature is composed of DuPont-associated members. As Nader has remarked: "The wealth and power of the family dynasty have not escaped public notice, but they escaped detailed public study." *The Company State,* the Nader Group's 845-page report released in December 1971, attempts to remedy that. The report was eighteen months in preparation by a seven member Task Force that canvassed the state of Delaware and Company. James Phelan and Robert Pozen directed the study.

Four reasons were offered to explain why he had sent his group to profile Delaware and DuPont. First, DuPont is a huge company operating in a relatively small area, affording researchers a chance to study the relationship more easily than they would with a company scattered across the country. Second, Nader felt DuPont was no stranger to the password "corporate responsibility," having controlled Delaware for decades. Third, techniques that DuPont was using and had used to enforce its position would be historically accessible. Finally, the way DuPont conducted itself in community affairs could also be easily explored.

The Task Force was not met with open arms by DuPont. The company made it sticky for employees to be interviewed on their own time. While they were being interviewed at work, they were accompanied by a company lawyer, a public relations man, and a tape recorder. The lawyer vetoed any questions which he considered to be of a sensitive nature. This environment was hardly conducive to employee candidness, precisely the effect the company sought to achieve. Questions sent to DuPont in writing were ignored or returned with "Confidential" on them, even when the Nader Group considered the questions to be of only a perfunctory nature. Tours were arranged through certain areas of company plants but the researchers could not speak to employees in the lunchroom. Despite these prohibitions, many employees spoke anonymously to the Task Force. Over 500 interviews were obtained with DuPont workers and directors, members of the DuPont family, lawyers, leaders of the black and white communities, physicians, politicians, developers, educators, reporters, architects, and social workers.

The Nader group recommended that the control of corporate policy be leavened by adding at least three public interest directors to the DuPont Board. To assess the effect of DuPont on each community, the report said it would be beneficial for standing local advisory committees to be set up in order to act as a conduit to the community for DuPont's plans, for DuPont's information dispersal leaves quite a bit to be desired on matters such as its minority employment figures, data on pollution and the results of product research.

It was felt that the employees should not be forced to donate to DuPont-designed charities. To prevent abuses in this area, the group thought that possibly laws might be passed making it illegal for corporations to give to charities. Or conversely, contributions would still be allowed but the corporations would get no tax deductions. Other recommendations included: the DuPont Air and Water Resources Committee, in addition to employees, should include local citizens; in its business with subcontractors, DuPont should require that they follow the pollution standards that the company itself follows; crews performing the work should be racially integrated.

DuPont employees are under the company's thumb. If a man is too outspoken, he can be replaced and his chances of landing a similar job in the Delaware area are slim. The report strongly urged that white collar employees, who now work without employment contracts, organize themselves into unions for protection. Employee grievance procedures should be revamped so that management does not have the final word, perhaps via the use of a neutral agency. Patents which DuPont employees develop while working for the company should revert to the inventor after a number of years if the company does not choose to make use of them. Pension plans, medical and life insurance, and bonuses all need upgrading, according to the report. For blue collar workers, a union or system of unions with more power is badly needed to help end the paternalism that currently exists.

To break up concentration of DuPont wealth in Delaware the Raiders recommended that the state income tax become "effectively progressive" in the upper tax echelons. Capital gains should be treated as ordinary incomes.

Private schools were noted as another means of promoting the wide social class disparity in the state. For economic sanctions, it envisioned no tax deductions be allowed for contributions to private schools. "If families choose not to avail themselves of free public education, the government should not subsidize their social preferences." Private clubs were mentioned as providing "a hidden form of decision-making" and were not an incentive to provide public recreation facilities. "DuPont family members should donate most of their land for public parks rather than for elitist private clubs." The report urged the state civil rights commission and the state attorney general to curb the "worse types of membership discrimination."

Delaware is so kind to corporations that the country's top 100 companies now make their corporate homes in Delaware. Among the residents besides DuPont are General Motors, Ford, IT&T and several large bank holding companies. Consequently, legal services are constantly in demand in order to help with the setting up of charters as well as maintaining them. To cut down on sophisticated "ambulance chasing," the Nader group had many specific suggestions. First, a Federal incorporation law which would charter corporations is needed. The March 11, 1972 issue of the *New Republic* had an article by Nader in which he advocated this very idea. He proposed that the top 1,000 corporations be Federally chartered, providing "new conditions for corporate democracy affecting shareholders and employees." In addition, directors would have to make any possible conflict of interest public, information would be more accessible about the corporation's activities, and anti-monopoly control would also be easier. This proposal sounded like it should interest only lawyers, but he claimed the average consumer had a stake in this too, especially in the way corporate bodies act in relation to government, the environment, and their own employees. Exemplifying one particular series of dubious affairs conducted for a member of the DuPont family, *The Company State* asked lawyers to take a hard look at their activities, especially when asked by their clients to provide quasi-legal service. Lawyers should also be granted time to engage in *pro publico bono* work for Delaware's minorities and poor people. Existing legal aid and public defense programs should be expanded. The Delaware Bar was criticized for its excessive interest in corporate affairs. It was urged to devote more time to consumers, criminal cases, the poor and juveniles.

DuPont has a sizeable voice in what is said about it,

since it owns both of Delaware's major newspapers. The Nader group found this intolerable. There is only one solution, said the Task Force: DuPont must divest itself of both the *Evening Journal* and the *Morning News*. Certainly the DuPonts do not need the revenue which is generated by the two papers.

DuPont reaction to the report was predictable. Its president, Charles B. McCoy, called the report "completely one-sided" and "negative." Irene DuPont, a company vice-president, remarked "I don't believe there is DuPont family control of Delaware." Representative Pierre DuPont took a softer line: "Many of the problems discussed in the report are problems of the corporate system in general. Perhaps they are exaggerated in our case because Delaware is so small."

The property tax, when misapplied, can become an easy enemy of consumers and an ally of business. Since the fall of 1970, a group in Nader's Public Interest Research Group has been carefully monitoring developments around the country concerning the levying of the property tax. To aid the establishment of consumer communication, a monthly newsletter detailing property tax developments around the country has been published since October, 1970.

Nader has been goading Senator Edmund Muskie, chairman of the Subcommittee on Intergovernmental Relations, to hold property tax hearings. The chiding has gone on for over a year and the hearings were scheduled at last for April, 1972. In a letter to Muskie, Nader said, "Since your announcement, the need for such hearings has become increasingly more urgent. Exposures of illegality and abuse in the administration of the property tax have accelerated and the magnitude of the tax burden falling as a result on unfavored taxpayers appears even greater than it did before." Nader went on to list what he felt were the six specific property tax abuses:

1) U.S. Steel in Gary, Indiana, is thought to be underassessed to the tune of about 110 million dollars. U.S. Steel refuses to disclose its capital investments and depreciation schedules, allowing it, in fact, to set its own tax.

2) In Chicago, U.S. Steel and its steel brethren avoid millions of dollars in taxes yearly. A group called the Citizens Against Pollution (CAP) has estimated this under-assessment at 16.4 million dollars. CAP also estimates that First National Bank of Chicago is paying only fifty-six percent of its proper share of taxes.
3) Maine loses over a million dollars annually from incorrect assessment of its timberlands. The state recently paid $125 per acre to acquire land assessed at $14 per acre. The firm that prepared the assessment also works for the timber companies.
4) In Augusta, Georgia, an industry-favoring development committee set a rate of one-eighth that paid by present industry in an effort to attract new industry. A taxpayer's suit voided this arrangement.
5) California loses about 250 million dollars annually in property taxes by virtue of state laws which are supposed to encourage the conservation of farm and agricultural land. Actually, it makes it all the more profitable for speculators to wait and get their price.
6) Throughout the Appalachian region, mineral land rights and equipment are consistently under-assessed and under-taxed. In one five-county area this came to $350,000 yearly, according to a citizen's group.

The cases of property tax abuse would probably fill a separate volume, but perhaps the enumeration of one such case would graphically highlight the problem throughout the country.

On May 14, 1971, Joseph Carini, the mayor of Wallingford, Connecticut wrote to Ralph Nader asking him to look into a recent reassessment which had greatly stirred the townspeople. Nader demurred, saying he really didn't have the resources to undertake such a project. However, the townsfolk were so persistent that Donald K. Ross, one of Nader's PIRG organizers and co-author of *Action for A Change* decided to look into the situation. He took along with him Brent English from the Connecticut Citizen Action Group. Neither was a trained real estate appraisor.

The townspeople were confronted with a tax reassessment that had recently cut industry's taxes from thirty-eight percent to twenty-three percent of the town's taxroll. This event came about after appeals from the industries were made. Nine out of eleven had their taxes reassessed (eighty-two percent of industry in Wallingford) while only eighty of a possible 574 homeowners (a mere fourteen percent) had any lowering of their burden.

The two investigators looked at specific aspects of the problem, beginning with United Appraisal Company of East Hartford, Connecticut which was responsible for the reappraisals. Though obviously on the face of things industry was favored, English and Ross noted, "frankly, we could not prove this point conclusively, so it remains an open question."

The second part of their investigation concerned the Wallingford town assessor, Robert Kemp. Kemp, who was also an officer of an appraisal firm that was a direct competitor of United Appraisal, proved to be less than the taxpayer's favorite man. By law, the assessment records were to be made public. However, Mr. Kemp allegedly absented himself when convenient. He just wasn't around much of the time. One woman signed an affidavit stating that in an effort to have her assessment re-evaluated she had made a dozen fruitless visits to Mr. Kemp's office. Would-be interviewers were told that he was out, and were not given a time when he might be in. Yet Mr. Kemp received wages as a full-time employee. Other people were not permitted to duplicate assessment records, although they are considered public information. Instead, they were told to hand-copy the material needed.

Wallingford is hardly the model of citizen redress. Ross and English filed a letter of complaint about Kemp with the International Association of Assessment Officers.

As Radph Nader said in the March 5, 1972 issue of the *New Republic:* "There is also no reason why a progressive property tax, as used in Australia, can't be used to help smaller property owners. Finally, procedures for easy and quick property-tax appeals should be established."

The citizens of Wallingford would agree.

One of Nader's earliest battles after his joust with GM was national gas pipeline safety, an area which does not affect public welfare until an accident occurs, and people are injured or killed and property destroyed. There are some 800,000 miles of gas transmission and distribution pipeline in this country which transmit gas under extreme pressure, up to 1,300 pounds per square inch. A leak or rupture can easily lead to a serious explosion. Some of the lines are in sparsely populated areas reaching hundreds of miles; others supply schools, factories, and private homes.

Among the conditions that should be cause for concern are corrosion, poor welding, placing the pipe too close to ground level, and thin and easily rupturable pipe. Nader stressed the need for good pipe, properly installed and regularly inspected. He cited the instance of a piece of pipe outside of St. Louis which had been dug up and brought to a Congressional hearing. The pipe had numerous small holes in it, and a too-large opening had been stuffed with cloth as a remedial measure.

In a fifteen-year period ending in 1965, industry sources told the Federal Power Commission that there had been sixty-four deaths and 222 injuries attributable to gas pipeline accidents. Nader, however, was inclined to believe that the industry was understating the case. Seventy-five deaths resulted from gas explosions in just a two-year period since the 1965 study.

Nader once asked an interviewer this rhetorical question about the situation: "Must we, as in auto safety, point to a mountain of dead bodies before the Federal Government or industry takes even the most halting action? No industry should be granted the right to a free major disaster."

The bus industry has come under attack on two fronts by Nader and his operatives. Safety of bus passengers and the in-bed relationship of bus carriers with the ICC are the two aspects that Nader has devoted a large amount of attention to. The safety crusade closely parallels that of Nader's efforts in the consumer auto market. Due to limited resources, this campaign has not been as fully articulated as he would probably like, and certainly not been as fully publicized. The accusation is that Greyhound regrooves tires on the rear of its buses, therefore providing no more traction than if they were bald. In the rain, should a bus go careening around a corner, the driver will hit the brakes but the bus will skid instead of slowing down to a halt.

To back up his claim, Nader cited a May, 1967 accident in New Jersey where a bus plunged down a fifty-foot embankment, killing a seventy-three-year-old woman and injuring twelve other passengers. The Department of Transportation, upon consideration of the accident, recommended criminal prosecution, for New Jersey state troopers found that the tires were so bald the underneath canvas was visible. In Baker, California, a Greyhound bus collided with a passenger car and twenty occupants of the bus were killed. The bus had flipped over and the people inside burned to death because the bus had no safety exits and the fuel tank was extremely vulnerable. Greyhound is subject to a $1,000 fine, according to Nader—that's all. No other penal provisions are provided for by the law.

Further accusations are that the company put pressure on the National Highway Safety Bureau and UCLA to keep a critical report from being leaked to the public. The report criticized Greyhound safety design. A new design was in the offing, although improvement was ranked by Nader to be only a little better.

Nader tried to get statistical comparisons between Greyhound and Trailway's New York to Washington run and their accident rates. The Bureau of Motor Carriers in the Department of Transportation refused him such data, claiming it would serve no useful purpose. Nader thinks otherwise; the public has a right to know which line is less likely to have passengers dead at the end of the line. Better service should be rewarded with more business. Spurred by Greyhound's lack of response to his safety suggestions, Nader has suggested that a Congressional investigation be undertaken to examine the nature of the relationship between Greyhound and the Bureau of Motor Carriers. He feels that this relationship "amounts to a merger of business and government in a joint venture to protect each other and delude the public." Once again, business has usurped the prerogative of the consumer to expect to be protected by a government-funded agency. "Here again," Nader says, "we have the problem of a regulatory agency, whose duty is to protect the public, deciding that its first allegiance is to the industry."

In *The Interstate Commerce Omission,* Nader's Raiders took a less than sanguine look at how Greyhound and Trailways have salted away just about all the intercity bus transportation. The Raiders selected one incident to illustrate their point—a case in which it was proven that Greyhound was guilty of predatory practices in an attempt to force a merger. For many years the smaller carrier had provided service within a larger area serviced by Greyhound. The two companies had made arrangements so that their services were complementary and the passenger changing over to the other line suffered only a small amount of inconvenience. But the giant eventually decided it wanted the midget's small piece of the pie, too. It talked to the smaller company about a merger, but they were not amenable to the idea.

Greyhound then initiated what amounted to guerrilla warfare, calculated to drive the small bus company out of business. Greyhound changed its schedules so that a transferring passenger had a three-hour wait. Then Greyhound put on its own route through the area—a longer trip but still less time-consuming than the wait at the station. The small company appealed to the ICC, which stepped in and lectured Greyhound. Faced with ICC action, Greyhound took a different tack and came to terms with the other carrier. Concluded the Nader Task Force: "Similar reasoning can be applied to any ICC merger approval, and the ICC should exercise revoking powers whenever it appears the promises of the merging carriers have been in bad faith."

Nader told Eric Norden of *Playboy* that ". . . aviation safety will present serious challenges in the coming years because of the growing congestion not only in the skies, but at our airports," adding that some 1,200 people die in air crashes each year as against 50,000 on our highways. But as Nader wrote in *Holiday:* ". . . the intrinsic value of human life must never be subjected to the attrition of such comparisons."

His thorough and on-going campaign against the poor safety record of American automobiles was not lost on those in the aviation industry. When a Nader Raider named Jim Bruce called and wanted to visit with Richard L. Collins of *Flying* magazine, the aviation writer was understandably wary. "Quite honestly," conceded Collins, "the chip on my shoulder was in evidence as Nader's man walked up the sidewalk." But any rancor soon disappeared. "The chip left in a hurry," Collins continued. "Jim Bruce received his degree in areonautical engineering from Princeton, and although he is not a pilot, he displayed a thorough knowledge of general aviation safety factors—both from the practical and engineering standpoints." Collins went on to add that Bruce had done a great deal of homework in the area. He wanted to question the writer on specific subjects and had already talked to most of the knowledgeable people in the field. After Bruce left, Collins recorded this very favorable comment: "Jim had gathered his information in a calm, highly professional manner—hardly in the image of a sensation-seeking crusader."

Nader has directed his criticisms of commercial and general aviation at the problem of crashworthiness, noting that a great many people are killed after the crash from explosion, smoke, fire, asphyxiation, or from striking a fixed object inside the plane on impact.

Fuselage improvements are an aspect needing improvement along these lines. As Nader noted in *Holiday:* "With new materials and design principles, more of the energy can be absorbed at a controlled rate during the collapse of the fuselage, thereby reducing the energy levels experienced by the passengers."

Increasing seat strength has been another bone of contention. If the seat snaps off its foundation upon impact, the passenger is thrown up for grabs inside the airplane.

The airlines say that the strength Nader is looking for will increase the weight of the plane to dangerous levels. Nader's response is that ". . . FAA's John Swearinger claims he has solved this problem and can build a seat with four times the strength of present ones without requiring any added weight." Two other solutions to the seat-snap problem that engineers have under consideration are air bag or air pillow devices similar to those now being tested in automobiles, and rearward facing seats such as found in some commuter trains.

Approximately twenty-five percent of all fatalities are the result of fires following crashes. Nader has constantly urged the airlines to take steps to protect the fuel supply upon crash, pointing out that the Air Force has for the last few years used a method where nitrogen is pumped into emptied fuel space. Fuel films or emulsions, gels, or thickened fuels are also possibilities. The fiery blowups punctuating most crashes make a convincing argument for smoking being banned entirely from the planes. One of Nader's better supporting examples for this argument refers to a flight with 153 on board back in 1963, that began to burn before the plane even left the runway. Subsequent investigation proved a lighted cigarette butt as the cause.

The use of synthetic materials in the cabin has been a source of disturbance. When subjected to fire or intense heat, many of the materials release toxic gases which can quickly overcome and asphyxiate passengers. Also, the smoke generated from the combustion of such materials can obscure vision, delaying exit to safety.

The most severe criticism is reserved for the poor evacuation procedures and facilities that planes now have. The exits are too few in number, and poorly marked. He quotes former president of United Air Lines William Allan Patterson, who remarked disgustedly after watching a "typical" evacuation demonstration: "Invite me back—but next time I want to see old ladies in the aircraft, cripples and mothers with children, and then I want to see fire and smoke and confusion. Then, and only then, will I be able to comment on whether or not we are able to evacuate an aircraft within two minutes or less, as we are required by law." To aid passengers in finding their way around in the smoke and heat of a cabin fire, smoke hoods have been proposed. Based on the conclusions of tests held at the FAA's Aeromedical Institute in Oklahoma City, an FAA official has concluded that the hoods can increase the possibility of passenger survival.

Are the airlines responsive to his safety pleas? Nader doesn't think so. He has related one instance of how a major airline manufacturer treated a fatal crash. The company found in 1967 that a number of its planes sold to commercial carriers had inferior engines involving a defect which would cause the propeller to come loose, and thereby slashing the fuselage of the plane and causing a crash. The company did not inform the FAA. They waited until thirty-eight people were killed in a crash attributed to this specific defect. The fine was \$8,000—about \$200 per death—and they fought to have it lowered to half that amount. This is not the first time, according to Nader, that the defect had been noticed by the FAA. The company had been cited for irregularities 100 times before.

The slap on the wrist continually administered by the FAA makes it more commercially feasible to produce an inferior product and pay the consequences if caught, because the profit potential is enormous.

We know technical adjustments can be made. As Nader puts it: "The controversy is not so much about engineering as it is about economics and changing old habits in both government and industry, a difficult process at best."

Nader Versus The Federal Bureaucracy

"It is abundantly clear that our institutions, public and private, are not really performing their regulatory functions," Ralph Nader wrote in 1972. "They tend not to control power democratically, but to concentrate it, and to serve special interest groups at the expense of voiceless citizens."

And the voiceless citizens generally are pretty helpless against institutions, public and private. Their helplessness is often a direct result of fear, for even though the American people have been taught that ours is a government "of the people, for the people, and by the people," we still seem to have a nameless dread when facing the concept of a large, seemingly incomprehensible institution, such as a major hospital or the army. And we seem to be even more fearful when attempting to cope with the tangled affairs of the Federal regulatory bureaucracy.

But Ralph Nader doesn't suffer the same handicap. He wades in fearlessly where the ordinary citizen fears to tread, into a muddled and often unreasoning mishmash that passes for government agencies, unleashing his blunt, knowledgeable logic, attempting to shine some light into the dark corners. Some of his most noticeable achievements have been in this area. Among the foes Nader has taken on are: the Federal Trade Commission, the Food and Drug Administration, the Interstate Commerce Commission, the Civil Aeronautics Board, the National Air Pollution Board, the National Railroad Administration, the Atomic Energy Commission, and the Departments of Agriculture and Transportation.

And now it appears he—and his associates—have decided to take on an even more formidable foe: Congress.

When Nader was appearing before the Senate Commerce Committee in May of 1971, he scolded the senators for proposing still another "fraud" on consumers, an auto-repair measure which Nader considered too weak to be able to fulfill its promises. "The committee should know by now that no more than ten percent of what any consumer law tells the executive branch to do ever gets done. In some cases, the percentage is much less."

But it wasn't just that the proposed bill should be stronger, it was also that Congress itself shares complicity in the "deceptive packaging" because it enacts laws to protect the consumer, but then does not provide adequate appropriations or close supervision required to carry out the intent of the law, Nader said.

When a bill has reached its crescendo of public interest, and Congress has pushed some form of legislation through in response to this public interest, then the public forgets. But the industry lobbyists stick around long after to see that their special interests are solved. No one, he argues, is lobbying for the public, not even Congress.

"Coldly and with slide rule precision," Nader charged, the auto industry has produced automobiles that need repairs so often that it creates a multi-billion-dollar replacement market, "marked by enormous and monopolistic company mark-ups" on parts.

If, after being exposed to the auto industry's "massive thievery" and the auto industry's contempt for both the consumer and Congress "for the past five years, if this is the best legislation your political antennae permit you to come up with, then it is respectfully suggested that some of you who are most concerned take some time out to ponder, like Lucretius, on the nature of things relating to the corporate state of our times.

"If there are criminal penalties for the poor and deprived" when they break laws, he continued, "then there must be criminal penalties for the automobile industry when its executives knowingly violate standards designed to protect citizens from injuries and systematic fraud."

The bill in question at that dispute was introduced by Senator Philip A. Hart. It would require the industry to make vehicles that are more easily repaired and less easily damaged. After 1975, bumpers on cars would have to hold up in a crash of five mph, without damage. Other engineering changes would also be required. Nader's contention was that the measure was too weak because it provided no criminal action for violations and no specific funding level for enforcement. Also, he said, the measure left too much discretion in the hands of the Secretary of Transportation.

Reacting angrily to Nader's criticism, Senator Theodore Stevens of Alaska said that Nader was too critical and that he did not give any credit to American industry.

"Do you give credit to a burglar because he doesn't burglarize ninety-nine percent of the time?" Nader asked.

This and other charges which Nader has hurled at individual senators and Congress as a whole probably prepared the Senate, and caused no great ripple of surprise to run through those august halls when Nader and friends announced last November that a non-partisan year-long study of Congress would be undertaken. He wrote to senators and invited their "suggestions and cooperation."

Named the "Congress Project," Nader said that the study would enlist the cooperation of "hundreds of citizens in nearly every Congressional district. In its past and in its present, Congress has been a continuous under-achiever," Nader stated, but it is still the "best hope for reclaiming America." That is why, he said, the study should take place.

Abdicating its leadership role to the Executive branch and forgetting the separation of power between the executive and legislative branches of government are two glaring faults of Congress. The separation of power has "been so eroded that the rare assertion by Congress makes headline news."

The investigation would range, Nader said, "from an analysis of the electoral and campaign process, to individual profiles of members of Congress, to the internal workings of the legislature and its interaction with the executive branch and private constituencies."

Robert Fellmeth was named project director of the study. In discussing the project in March, 1972, Fellmeth said that there has been preliminary research which is necessary for the study, but the final research had not started as yet.

"A team of fifteen people have researched the law in specific areas, the law in lobbying, various tax loopholes, systems, and breaks that affect lobbying one way or another. They've researched a number of other questions and written a number of other memos which include explanation of the law, regulations, leading techniques in the field, major contracts, etc. . . . In terms of the status of the project, most of the people who have been recruited are at work. There are about fifty or sixty missing of the 535 [members in Congress] needed to be covered. All state capitols but one are covered . . . We have accepted about 100 of 110 people we want down here. They'll work part-time and full-time until the summer, then work full-time in the summer, and then back . . ."

Fellmeth said that when Nader suggested he lead the study, he decided that he couldn't pass up the opportunity. "It was going to be too important."

Among the other regulatory agencies which Nader has tackled is the Federal Trade Commission (FTC). He has been a hard taskmaster with that particular agency ever since 1968, when "Nader's Raiders" loosed upon the FTC the devastating charge that Paul Rand Dixon, then Commission chairman, had turned it into "a patterned and intricate deceptive practice unto itself."

The report was published just before Nixon took office in 1969. Instead of responding directly to the Nader indictment, Nixon, using his perfect technique of facing the issue squarely sideways, asked the American Bar

Association to conduct a fresh "study and professional appraisal of the FTC." It seemed the President could not bear the thought of appearing to give credit to the rollicking Nader's Raiders, but in ordering the Bar Association study, he did just that—sort of a back-handed compliment.

The study this time was headed by Miles Kirkpatrick, a Philadelphia anti-trust lawyer and chairman of ABA's anti-trust division. The ABA report completely confirmed the Nader study. The FTC should abolish its "several serious and pervasive deficiencies" in leadership, in staff, in policy, and in performance. The conclusion reached by the ABA study was that an immediate appointment of "an outstanding chairman" who was endowed with "sufficient strength and independence to resist pressures from Congress, the Executive Branch, or the business community that tend to cripple effective performance by the FTC."

Nixon followed the suggestion of the committee as far as appointing a new chairman, but whether Caspar Weinberger was "an outstanding chairman" was in question. Weinberger was associated with California Governor Reagan, and the appointment seemed to be merely a political face-lift, a sham. However, when Weinberger took over in January 1970, he began a vigorous housecleaning, restaffing and reorganizing of the FTC. He had hardly started, though, when he was given another government appointment and the chairmanship was again vacant.

Nixon pulled a big surprise. He appointed Miles Kirkpatrick to the position—the same man who headed the ABA study. It seemed that Nixon took the FTC's duties to the consumer seriously.

The FTC has been around a long time, since September 2, 1914. The purpose of the FTC in the beginning was to combat the huge trust combines which appeared in the 1800's. The trust movement became an issue in the 1912 Presidential election, and when Wilson was elected President, he called for Congress to pass new anti-trust legislation. Congress passed two laws dealing with the subject: The FTC act and the Clayton Act of 1914.

As a result of these and other laws, the "maintenance of

free competitive enterprise as the keystone of the American economic system became the objective to the work of the FTC," or so it is stated in the FTC brochure.

The Supreme Court has defined the task of the Commission as the prevention of practices which have a "dangerous tendency unduly to hinder competition or create a monopoly" or which are "opposed to good morals because [they are] characterized by deception, bad faith, fraud or oppression."

Nader is not always at odds with FTC, of course, and when they act as he feels they should, they receive a sort of tempered praise from him.

When the FTC accused the nation's four largest breakfast-cereal makers of "shared monopoly" in January 1972, and threatened to break them up into smaller, more competitive companies, Nader issued a statement congratulating the FTC and saying that the case, if pursued, could be "one of the most important developments in anti-trust enforcement in the last decade." He said that the shared monopolies or "oligopolies" of the sort alleged in the cereal case cost consumers twenty-three billion dollars a year in over-charges.

But mixed in with his praise was a mild slap. "In order to help the individual consumer realize a price saving which will be meaningful in terms of his annual personal budget," Nader said, "additional Commission complaints against other highly concentrated industries are necessary." He said that the automobile and steel industries were "obvious places to start."

The monopolistic practices mentioned in the FTC accusation were that the four largest breakfast-cereal makers—Kellogg Company, General Mills, Inc., General Foods Corp., and Quaker Oats Company—have used trademarks to conceal basic product similarities and have also used premiums to induce purchases; the result being "high barriers to entry into the ready-to-eat cereal market."

Other monopolistic practices alleged by the FTC to be used by the cereal makers are: controlling the allocation of shelf space and the selection and removal of cereal for display in retail groceries; acquiring competitive companies; failing to challenge one another's decisions to increase prices and in general following one another's price increases.

If the complaint is upheld, many other industries, including the steel and automobile industries mentioned by Nader, would be vulnerable to attack.

Other areas of the FTC's scope which have been influenced by Nader include the requiring of major advertisers, industry by industry, to submit documentation for such advertising as they use for public inspection. Automakers were first and their follow-ups are to be manufacturers of air conditioners and electric razors.

Robert Pitofsky, director of the FTC's Bureau of Consumer Protection, was asked if he appreciated Nader and the Nader groups.

"Our paths often cross. I don't generalize about the Nader operation because there are so many satellites and so many different people who have taken on the mantle of college of Ralph Nader, a spokesman for Ralph Nader, and I don't see all of them by any means. The ones that I have seen in this agency are very bright, committed, dedicated, able, young people. They do their homework. They don't come in here and expect that, just because their heart is in the right place, we'll do something they want us to do. They do come in with polished, sophisticated legal briefs and arguments. By and large, I think they make this agency more effective than if they weren't around."

Other Nader investigations of the Federal bureaucracy have touched the Atomic Energy Commission. In July, 1970, Nader asked his old "friend" Senator Muskie to investigate the AEC. In a letter to Muskie, he wrote that "the available indications are" that John W. Gofman and Arthur R. Tamplin, of the Lawrence Radiation Laboratory at Livermore, California, have been persecuted by the AEC. The two men delivered a series of technical papers criticizing the allowable radiation dosage limits set for nuclear power plants.

Nader said that Gofman and Tamplin appear to have been "accused of heresy by an agency so committed to the promotion of atomic energy that it has insisted that radiation risks be treated more as articles of faith to be intoned than propositions to be examined continually.

"The AEC has been known to obscure the risks, assuage the public and assume that public access and public evaluation of the benefits and costs of nuclear power technologies are deferrable luxuries."

And, of course, there are Nader's famous fights with the Highway Traffic Commission, which he helped create. But in Nader's continuing consumer campaign, this area of auto safety seems to be the one which has borne the most fruit. A news release from the public relations division of Ford Motor Company in April, 1972, stated that "as a result of the consumerism movement, car owners can expect significant improvements in automotive service in the decade ahead . . ." E. P. Williams, service programs manager of the Ford Customer Service Division, made these remarks at the Missouri Automobile Dealers Association convention. "Bridging the troubled waters of consumer discontent may be the toughest buyer mandate American business has ever received. But the smart businessman will make the adjustment called for because he always has. And to those retailers who fail to join him, his advice might be: "Seller Beware!"

To anybody who fails to heed the new public awareness advocated more by Ralph Nader than anyone else, the cry might be "Beware!" Well enough. For Nader will take on anybody or anything which is not fulfilling his or its potential—and who really does?

Certainly not the Bureau of Reclamation. In a task force report on the bureau, Nader wrote: "As the editor and co-authors, Richard Berkman and Kip Viscusi, analyze the Bureau's benefit-cost calculations, its cost overruns, its tunnel-vision inattention to devastating ecological consequence of its work and the need of impoverished Indians for water, they conclude that many of the Bureau's activities should be stopped, curtailed or redirected."

The original purpose of the Bureau was to build dams and irrigation canals and reclaim arid lands in the West, but in *Damning the West*, the authors reach the conclusion that "no longer is there a need for more and bigger dams and irrigation canals . . . Yet BuRec doggedly pursues this counterproductive goal that benefits politicians, bureaucrats, and a few profiteering irrigators, but not the nation as a whole."

And the nation as a whole is what Nader is most concerned with.

"We're reaching a point right now where it's becoming fashionable to attack Ralph Nader and I think that's going to increase. Some of it is press jealousy. But it's always news in the media when the boy bites the dog, so to speak. Another report coming out with Ralph Nader criticizing something is expected. So what becomes news is something being wrong with the report or its methods or him. This results in absurd kinds of media results," said Robert Fellmeth.

"For example, in California we devastingly documented a single 102 million-dollar California land fraud . . . hardly a mention of it anywhere. Instead there was a long front-page article on the fact that we did not interview the Attorney General Deputy O'Brien, . . . before we published a few sentences about him. Which, in fact, we had. The point is that the focus and intent was on us—personalities, not fact.

"It's as if there's no outside world—that everything is okay in America—that they're not doing anything to the land in California, the streams are perfectly clean and not being polluted, that people are not being poisoned with pesticides. These things are getting less and less attention while the question of our self-aggrandizing is getting more.

"We see increasing attention being given to us . . . and less and less to the issues that affect people's lives, and this is frustrating. That's a phenomenon that happens when you have a personality like Ralph Nader," Fellmeth said.

It's obvious that Ralph Nader is not going to fade out of the American scene quickly. As his critics grow in number so do his supporters. He is both loved and feared, not apparently as a man but as a consumer figure, an advocate of change. But not radical change either. For the more one learns of Ralph Nader as a public figure, the more one realizes that here is a traditionalist.

Ted Jacobs said it this way: "What Ralph is all about is very basic founding fathers stuff. The founding fathers saw one kind of power that was out of control in the world—political power—and they built a system that they thought would control unbridled power. The power that is out of control today is corporate power, and Ralph Nader is saying, 'Let's bring some democratic controls to bear on that.'" (to Blum in *Redbook,* November 1971.)

A patriot in the real sense of the word. Nader, in fact, has called for a "new kind of patriotism," which he defined in *Life* magazine. First, "patriotism must once again be rooted in the individual's conscience and beliefs." Second, "patriotism begins at home. Love of country in fact is inseparable from citizen action to make the country more lovable." Third, "if it is unpatriotic to tear down the flag . . . why isn't it more unpatriotic to desecrate the country itself—to pollute, despoil and ravage the air, land and water?" And fourth, "there is no reason why patriotism has to be so heavily associated . . . with military exploits, jets and missiles."

Nader must have agreed with President Kennedy's line, "Ask not what your country can do for you, ask what you can do for your country." And what you can do for your country, according to Nader, is to make it more lovable.

Everything Nader says is based on the responsibility of the citizen. Especially politics. "Politics is in such a low state of response it's necessary to go to the citizen to see if he'll wake up. Politics will improve when the citizen improves. Not only the average citizen, but the lawyer, doctor, teacher, engineer, the leaders as well as the followers."

He feels that there are already a lot of people in America who are ready to work for change, but they don't know how. And what he is out to do, is to develop "professional citizen skills" which he can then teach.

As part of that development of the "professional citizen," Nader has a new arm called Public Citizen, Inc. He formed the company in 1971 to help finance his public-interest operations. Through direct mail campaigns and newspaper ads, Nader asked for contributions from the public.

"Dear Fellow Citizen:" the ad began, "Imagine that twenty-five or thirty years ago citizens concerned about the future quality of life in America had gotten together to do something about it." And the ad ends with this note: "Let it not be said by a future, forlorn generation that we wasted and lost our great potential because our despair was so deep we didn't even try, or because each of us thought someone else was worrying about our problems." And it's signed "Sincerely, Ralph Nader."

The appeal worked. In March 1972, Nader announced that the Public Citizen, Inc. had received contributions of $640,000 in the first seven months. After advertising and other expenses were deducted, there was a net of $462,230.

The funds collected thus far were to be used to finance his also recently formed Retired Professionals Action Group and three other operations—The Health Research Group, The Tax Reform Research Group, and a litigation group. In addition, Public Citizen was contributing $10,000 to the Center for Women Policy Studies, which will operate independently of Nader and will advocate women's rights in employment, education and other areas.

Women's rights is an area that Nader has been interested in for some time. In 1971 he said that he felt that women were oppressed and are oppressors at the same time. He said this was because they had to live by their wits, and had learned to "rule" their husbands by nagging and henpecking. "But more important is the way they've been basically segregated. Isn't it a tell-tale sign that less than one percent of engineers and only five percent of lawyers are women?"

One woman who believes in Nader is New York writer and Women's Liberation advocate, Gloria Steinem, who touted Nader for President in a *New York* magazine article. She had found that on college campuses Ralph Nader was the one speaker whom the students and teachers alike admired and respected. "He's the only totally honest man I've ever met," one Seton Hall student was reported to have told Ms. Steinem. "But what impressed us all most was that he really believes this country can be saved, and that we can do it. He gave us something *real* to do, something that affects our lives, not just the manufactured, useless projects everybody else gives us."

Steinem concluded her article with this thought, ". . . The American Dream has to do with goods and services for all, and that dream is failing. Wouldn't a Consumer Crusader be just the man to save us?"

Gore Vidal in an *Esquire* magazine article also praised Ralph Nader and said he should be President. But what does Nader, himself, think of this?

Nothing doing, he says. "I am not interested in any form of political office, appointive or elective."

He then returns to his favorite and most impressive theme—the idea of citizen power.

"If," he says, "this form of government of ours is to be more responsive, it's got to be preceded by a new form of citizen and community action, such as environmental groups, consumer groups, tenant groups, poverty groups, those kinds of groups."

Politics today "is a mirror image. What you see on one side is a set of powerful lobbyists and on the other side a set of abdicating citizens. That's what equals politics today."

And no longer, *no longer,* should there be abdicating citizens. "There's got to be a new kind of career—full-time citizenship."

Nader and Nader's associates are constantly exploring new citizen responsibilities: The investigation of Congress, a definitive study of nuclear power for consumers, and the continuing advocacy of greater roles by lawyers, doctors, engineers and other professions.

Another sideline of Nader's is attacking youth. "I have never seen a softer generation," he told some health and medical students. "I have never seen one described as soft as this generation."

Certainly, softness is not one of Nader's character traits. Neither softness nor faint-heartedness. He wades into arenas where the battle is toughest, but where the rewards are highest. He hasn't always won—not what he went after, but he has managed to focus public attention on problems that went unheeded for too long. He has awakened the American citizen to his proper role in the government. And has proven beyond a doubt that you can fight city hall. The consumer movement he has started is going to be difficult, if not impossible to stop—if, indeed, anyone who really thought about it would really want to.

What Ralph Nader does in the future isn't that important. Obviously, he will do something, and probably something which will benefit all of us.

What is important is what we as citizens do in the future. And how much we really care about our own well-being.

Bibliography

Buckhorn, Donald; *Nader: The People's Lawyer* (New York, Prentice-Hall, 1972)

Bruce, Ronald, Editor; *The Consumer's Guide To Product Safety* New York, Award Books, 1971)

Council On Economic Priorities, The; *Efficiency In Death: The Manufacturers Of Anti-Personnel Weapons* (New York, Perennial Library, 1970)

Cox, Edward F., Robert C. Fellmeth, John E. Schulz; *Nader's Raiders* (New York, Grove Press, 1970)

Cross, Jennifer; *The Supermarket Trap* (New York, Berkley Medallion Book, 1971)

Esposito, John C.; *Vanishing Air* (New York, Grossman, 1970)

Fallows, James M.; *The Water Lords* (New York, Bantam, 1971)

Fellmeth, Robert; *The Interstate Commerce Omission* (New York, Grossman, 1970)

Lasson, Kenneth; *The Workers* (New York, Grossman, 1971)

McCarry, Charles; *Citizen Nader* (New York, Saturday Review Press, 1972)
Marine, Gene and Judith Van Allen; *Food Pollution: The Violation Of Our Inner Ecology* (New York, Holt Rinehart Winston, 1972)
Nader, Ralph; *Unsafe At Any Speed* (New York, Grossman, 1965)
Nader, Ralph, Lowell Dodge, Ralf Hotchkiss; *What To Do With Your Bad Car: An Action Manual For Lemon Owners* (New York, Bantam, 1971)
Peterson, Mary Bennett; *The Regulated Consumer* (Los Angeles, Nash, 1971)
Townsend, Claire; *Old Age: The Last Segregation* (New York, Bantam, 1971)
Turner, James S.; *The Chemical Feast* (New York, Grossman, 1970)
Zwick, David and Marcy Benstock; *Water Wasteland* (New York, Grossman, 1971)